S0-BSH-562

DATE DUE

"When I get out," he says, "I want to go live on a farm in the forest. That's the only way I can stay out of trouble. There's too much happening in Chicago." But it is a lie he tells to himself. At nineteen, he has never seen a forest. The only farms he knows are the flat black fields that stretched away from the road as the black prison bus drove him the sixty-five miles from the Chicago area to rural Pontiac, Illinois. He is a child of what black sociologist E. Franklin Frazier once aptly called "the city of destruction." Probed and processed by the psychologists of the Illinois penitentiary system, he has already been classified a "doubtful" for rehabilitation. He has entered the no-exit world of prison, parole, the streets, and, perhaps, prison again.

—From the Prologue

THE
JUSTICE
MACHINE

The People vs. Donald Payne

Don Holt

BALLANTINE BOOKS • NEW YORK
An Intext Publisher

Copyright © 1972 by Newsweek, Inc.

All rights reserved.

SBN 345-02495-8-125

Part of this material previously appeared in Newsweek
Magazine. © 1971 by Newsweek, Inc.

This edition published by arrangement with Newsweek,
Inc.

First Printing: April, 1972

Printed in the United States of America

Cover photo by Jeff Lowenthal

BALLANTINE BOOKS, INC.
101 Fifth Avenue, New York, N.Y. 10003

Prologue: The Farm in the Forest

Donald Payne sits on the front third of a wooden prison chair, slouching gracefully, his spidery legs straight out. His prison denims are creased and clean, the shirt is unbuttoned. He is nonchalant, cool, detached. "When I get out," he says, "I want to go live on a farm in the forest. That's the only way I can stay out of trouble. There's too much happening in Chicago." But it is a lie he tells to himself. At nineteen, he has never seen a forest. The only farms he knows are the flat black fields that stretched away from the road as the black prison bus drove him the sixty-five miles from the Chicago area to rural Pontiac, Illinois. He is a child of what black sociologist E. Franklin Frazier once aptly called "the city of destruction." Probed and processed by the psychologists of the Illinois penitentiary system, he has already been classified a "doubtful" for rehabilitation. He has entered the no-exit world of prison, parole, the streets, and, perhaps, prison again.

It was a swift, sudden passage. A year before, Donald Payne was just another black school dropout. Out of work and on the streets, he was a lanky, sullen kid who liked to sleep late, wear zesty clothes, drink beer, and shoot some pool.

Then came the night of August 4, 1970. Donald Payne was swept into the system of American justice and processed through. The police report tells it simply:

". . . At 2100 (9 P.M.), Aug. 4, 1970 . . . victim stated that two male Negroes entered his store and the taller of the two came out with a gun and announced that this is a holdup. . . . With this the victim . . . walked away from the area of the cash register. When he did this, the smaller offender shouted, 'Shoot him.' The taller offender aimed the pistol at him and pulled the trigger about two or three times. The weapon failed to fire. The offenders then fled. . . ."

It was a botched job—nobody was hurt and nothing stolen—and so Payne was, in one sense, only another integer in the numbing statistics of American crime.

But the case of the People vs. Donald Payne was in another sense central to the malaise of the nation's decaying big cities. Street crime has contributed powerfully to that malaise—and street crime in urban America has become in large and growing measure black crime. The subject has until lately been thought too painful for public discussion; to raise it has been considered treasonable among blacks and racist among sympathetic whites. But the statistics command attention. One little-noted staff study for Lyndon Johnson's Commission of Violence showed arrest rates ten to twenty times higher for blacks than for whites in serious crimes of violence; another, a seventeen-city survey, found blacks implicated in 72 percent of the criminal homicides, 74 percent of the aggravated assaults, 70 percent of the rapes, and 85 percent of the robberies marked solved by police. To acknowledge these figures is only to recognize the damage done blacks by years of poverty and discrimination. To suppress them is to ignore not only the fears of white people but the pain of the blacks who are the victims of the vast majority of black crime.

Donald Payne's passage from stickup to stationhouse to jail to court and finally into prison says more than any law text or flow chart about the realities of crime and punishment in America. The quality of justice in Chicago is neither very much better nor very much worse than in any major American city. The agents of justice in Chicago are typically overworked, understaffed, disconnected, case-hardened, and impossibly rushed. Payne protested his innocence to them every step of the way, even after he pleaded guilty. There is, given the evidence, no compelling reason to believe him, and no one did—least of all the lawyer who represented him. So the agents of justice handed him and his case file along toward a resolution that satisfied none of them wholly. "That we really have a criminal justice system is a fallacy," says University of Chicago law professor Hans Mattick. "What we have is a case-disposition system." In the winter of 1970–71, the system disposed of the People vs. Payne—and the sum of Donald Payne's case and tens of thousands more just like it across the nation is the real story of justice in America.

1. Donald

He was one kid at home and another in the street. Donnie-at-home was straight—nice-mannered, his stepfather said. Puttering with a radio. Punning with the family. Church on Sunday—*well, maybe next Sunday*—and school on Monday, sometimes. But Donald-in-the-street was cool. Six-one and sharp: sky-blue suit, white-stitched matching brown shirt and tie, brown side-buckle loafers, hair growing out in an Afro an inch and a half high. Walking that liquid walk—*diddybop diddybop*—and talking that languid talk. Shucking on the corner, jiving with the chicks, messing with the man. *Everybody do something wrong sometime*. Cool.

They fought over Donald Payne, home against street, a war of the worlds recapitulated ten thousand times every day in the ghetto; only when you live in a ghetto you can never get far enough away from the street to be sure of the outcome. Payne's mother tried. Her first husband left her and their four kids when Donnie, the youngest, was still little. But she kept them together and, thirteen years ago, was remarried to Cleophilus Todd, a dark, rumbly voiced man who preaches Sundays in the storefront Greater Mount Sinai M.B. Church and works weekdays to keep his family and his ministry afloat. Payne's mother

4

bore two more children, and worked some of the time; and two years ago they were able to put enough together to escape the gang-infested section where Donald grew up and move into a little green-and-white frame house in a fringe working-class neighborhood called Roseland.

The house is lace-curtain Negro, carpeted and overstuffed and sunny; there is a Martin Luther King souvenir plate on one living-room wall and, on another, an ornately framed mirror with china figurines on shelves and a motto at the top—HAVE FAITH IN GOD.

But it may have come too late for Donald. He had already begun sliding out of school; it bored him—*They'd be repeatin' the same things over and over again, goin' over the same thing, the same thing*—so he started skipping, and when the school called about him he would pick up the phone and put it back on the hook without saying anything. *Maybe I thought it was too much happenin' out there in the streets to be goin' to school.* Or church either. "They have to go to church long as they live with us," says Cleophilus Todd. For years, Donald did; he spent his Sunday mornings in the peeling blue-curtained storefront, shouting gospel in the choir, listening to his stepfather demanding repentance of a little congregation of women and small children in the mismatched second-hand pews and hardwood theater seats. But it got claustrophobic on Mount Sinai. *I just slowed down. I started sayin' I'd go next Sunday, and then I wouldn't. And then I just stopped.* The street was winning. There were conflicts deep in Donald that neither he nor his mother nor Todd really understood. His nice manner around the house was often a façade his parents chose to accept. It was easier that way. If Donald cared to face it, he found home oppressive, his mother domineering. *She tries to tell me what to do*. It was not the kind of life he wanted. Todd was no model for him either. *He's just a preacher. All he does is go to church*. And, even more degrading— *He just treats me like a kid*. It was his own father, who had remarried and lived not far away, whom Donald came more and more to admire. Something of a swinger in Donald's mind, the older Payne wore sharp clothes and *has young ideas*. He saw him infrequently, but came to feel that *he's the only one who understands me, he treats me like an adult*.

Donald Payne showed a knack for electricity; he made a couple of lamps and a radio in the school shop before he stopped going, and brought them home to his mother. She would ask him why he didn't think about trade school. "He could fix everything from a light to a television set," she says. "He was fine as long as he was busy. Only time you had to worry about him was when he had nothin' to do." Which was often. He never ran with gangs; he was too much of a loner for that.

But he spent a lot of idle hours with this friend and then that, down on the beach in summers (he bragged he drank four quarts of beer every day), in the corner pool room, or shooting dice in a hallway or alley. He did work sometimes, two jobs at once for a while, and once he talked to a man working on a house about how to get into electrical work. The man told him about apprenticeships and gave him the address of his union far across town. *But I just hated to travel. It bored me even when I was workin'—I just hated to take that trip. So I kept puttin' it off and puttin' it off.* Donald looked down. He was, at the moment he told the story, handcuffed to a chair in the Criminal Courts building. *And then this.*

And then this. Nobody knows, really, why the street swallows up so many of them. Poverty in the midst of affluence is surely part of it, and color in the midst of whiteness; so are heroin and broken homes and the sheer get-it-now impulsiveness of life in so empty and so chancy a place as a ghetto. No one can say which ones will go wrong —why Donald Payne, for example, will get into big trouble while brothers and sisters may not. "I told 'em all," says Todd, "I'm not going to be spending all my time and money on jail cases for you doing something you don't need to get into."

But Donald did get into it. He is an oddly detached and distant youth—so much of substance slithered right around him, leaving hardly a trace. Later on, testing in prison would show him to be of average intelligence but "seriously underdeveloped." The schools carried his name on the rolls through his sixteenth birthday, but in prison he tested out at just barely the fourth-grade level. He was classified functionally illiterate, something he was not willing to admit even to himself.

Thus his responses grew to be very basic: what he saw, he wanted. And the context of everything, his own life, his past and future, was very fuzzy. *I like money,* he would say. *I like clothes, I like to party. I like money in my pocket.* A prison psychologist later marked him down as having adopted an "irresponsibly hedonistic approach to life," and went on to make the chilling prediction that he would "use the quickest means possible to achieve his needs."

That, of course, was based on the history of a court conviction. Could anyone have quessed earlier? Donald growing up had at least avoided one source of trouble—the fighting gangs, the Black P Stone Nation (nee the Blackstone Rangers) or the Disciples or the Gangsters were not for him. *I don't indulge in such activities*, he says with a mocking formality, and pals from the block confirm it. Still, he did get run in a few times for disorderly conduct, a routine hazard for kids in the ghetto street. And in 1968 he was busted for burglary.

It was a kid-stuff filling-station job, two tires and a sign, and Payne was caught with the tires, one under each arm, a few blocks away. He insisted he was only trying to help a friend sell them, but Todd says he confessed to the family. And later on, in prison, he would relate that he had gone to the gas station that morning to buy tires but didn't have enough money. That night he he came back for them, but, he excuses himself, he was "intoxicated" and didn't know what he was doing. He wound up pleading guilty in a deal for a few days in jail and two years on probation. It came to little: probation in theory is a means to rehabilitation but probation offices in fact, in Chicago and around the country, tend to have too many cases and too little time to do much active rehabilitating. Payne's papers were lost for several months until he finally got scared and came in to find out why no one had called him. After that, he reported once every month, riding two hours on buses to see his probation officer for ten minutes. *We talked about was I workin' and how was I doin' out on the street*—that was all. Once the probation man referred him to a job counselor. Payne never went, and no one seems to have noticed. He got nothing, really, from probation. Except he violated it. And later on the parole board would take a very dim view of that: the first group of officials to pay much attention to the matter. Because in the middle of the summer of 1970, at eighteen, he got into big trouble.

Meeting Donald Payne, handcuffed in his chair, one is struck first by the remnants of the child: the shy flicking eyes, the dark slash of acne, the bravado tilt of the head, the low loose-jointed slouch, the habit of blaming all his past, present, and future difficulties on somebody else. *I have no say-so over it*. But there are uncomfortable glimpses of the man as well: the flicking-eyes challenge, the half-smile dares, the manner says, *I'm cool, I'll be back*. The people Payne met in his progress through the system saw it and put it down as scorn, or belligerence, or braggadocio, or just plain trouble. Or maybe it was the victory of the street. *Maybe it was too much happenin' out there*: maybe what was happening was boys imitating men in a community where all too many of the men are all too visibly defeated. "Donnie was one child I never really knew what to do with," his mother says; one wonders now whether there can be a second chance.

2. The Victim

A voice said, "I want that." Joe Castelli looked up from the till, and there across the counter stood this stringy black kid with an insolent grin and a small-caliber blue-steel automatic not four feet from Castelli's face. Castelli can't remember what he thought in that split second; maybe it was how he had worked behind that counter for twenty-four years and how all of it was slipping away. *The colored are driving me out.* The thought haunts him still, and so does the image of that pistol. And now, sometimes, Joe Castelli wants to kill somebody.

Castelli was twenty-four when he went to work for Shop-Rite Liquors, a sawed-off Italian kid clerking in a mostly Irish section on Chicago's South Side.* He worked the counter for fourteen years, then—when the owner decided to retire—scraped together the money to buy the store and the connecting neighborhood bar. It seemed to have a lot of advantages. The store was on a busy commercial street dotted with other small businesses and a block and a half west of a major north-south artery. Though the building was old,

*The original names of Castelli, his store, and his clerk have all been changed at his request.

the first floor provided ample room for display, a warehouse and big cooler in the back, and a long U-shaped bar in the next room. He installed flashing blue, white, and orange lights and a big electric display sign outside, brightened the interior with fluorescents and pink paint, and stocked his supermarket-style shelves with bread, milk, and canned goods along with the booze and beer. His trade was mostly with the old Irish—the cops, the firemen, the sanitation workers. "Real family people," he says. "They come in and buy one or two quarts of beer. I can count the number of fights we've had in here on one hand."

He never worried much about robberies either. "That's the reason," he will tell visitors, pointing to an arch in the pink wall. The old dirty wooden floor goes uphill as it approaches the opening and then disappears into the darkness of the barroom. "They don't know who could come out of there. The other room makes them nervous."

The one successful robbery occurred in 1948. Two armed white men herded everyone, including young Joe Castelli and two very frustrated detectives, into the cooler. Then, four years ago, two blacks came in. One stood watch at the front door. But Castelli yelled and a clerk came pumping out of the archway. The two ran off.

Still, all those years Castelli was only dimly aware of what was happening. Now, suddenly, it all seems to be closing in on him. He is forty-eight, going gray and thickening around the middle, and he has begun thinking ten years ahead to his own retirement. But his options seem to him suddenly narrowed by blind demographic forces he can neither control nor completely comprehend—by the quickening scramble of the blacks south and west out of the brawling, gang-ridden ghetto called Englewood. Castelli's store is on the west side—the white side—of the north-south artery, Ashland Avenue, that held for some years as a boundary between the races. Now that thin divide is crumbling: the younger whites have begun pulling out, abandoning the trim frame houses and two-family houses to the first upwardly mobile blacks and the last aging Irish whose lives and fortunes are sunk in their homes. The neighborhood is "changing," and Castelli doesn't like it. "You can't cope with the colored," he says, a frown darkening his round brown eyes. "They're animals. Animals."

The blacks, like Castelli himself, are only struggling for air, but the view from behind the counter is a narrow and a bitter one; urban crime counts more there than urban sociology. The thrice-told tales fly endlessly between Castelli and his clerk, Fred DeAngelo, a chain-smoking man of fifty-eight with stained fingers and a narrow, leathery face. Tales of the black kids whose only ID is their jail discharge papers. The teen-ager who flared menacingly, *"What you mean?"* when Joe amiably called him "lad." The one who lugged a whole case of Scotch into the cooler, emptied it into a shopping bag, and walked out. ("The police stopped him," DeAngelo says, "but all they did was kick him in the pants and send him back across Ashland.") The one who filched a bottle, set it on the counter, laid a machete alongside it, and asked for a bag to wrap it in. The one who came in every day to buy a can of beer and steal a fifth of Scotch. The endless petty pilfering. "They stick a bottle in here"—Castelli tugged out the waistband of his trousers in front and dropped an imaginary fifth inside—"and all you can do is take it out of their pants. We maybe have that four times a day —we don't even know. These men can go to ten, twenty, thirty stores a day, and you gotta take the loss."

And finally the gangly black kid with the blue-steel .25 and the frightening half-smile—the kid Castelli identified later as Donald Payne. He and another, smaller, youth came in the OUT door that mild August evening, just as Castelli was stuffing two hundred and fifty or three hundred dollars in receipts from cash register No. 2 into his pockets. "I want that," the tall one said. Castelli edged away. "Shoot him! Shoot him!" the small one yelled. The tall kid stared at Castelli and poked the gun across the counter at him. "You mother-fucker," he said. He squeezed the trigger, maybe once, maybe two or three times.

The gun went *click*.

The two kids turned and ran. Castelli started after them, bumped against the end of the counter, and went down. He got up and dashed outside, but the youths disappeared down a dark alley. An old white man emptying garbage saw them go by. The tall one pointed the pistol aloft and squeezed again. This time it went off.

A woman customer in a liquor store across the street came over and told Castelli she had seen the boys earlier getting out of a black Ford. Castelli found the car parked nearby and wrote down the

license number. The driver—a third black youth
—followed him back to the store. "What you taking my license for?" he demanded. "I was just
waiting for my wife—I took her to the doctor." He
stood there yelling for a while, but some of
Castelli's white neighbors crowded into the store
and the black youth left. Castelli went back into
the street, flagged down an unmarked police car
he recognized and handed over the number, and
the hunt was on.

Castelli made some changes after that. He
closed off one of the two doors. He rearranged the
floor plan so that all the liquor was behind the
counter; only food in the self-service area up
front. And he laid in some hardware. The night
of the holdup, he says ruefully, "I had a pistol, far
away. Now I got a couple close. Very close."

He reports this with a faint edge of surprise. "I
don't want to live like that," he says. "I don't want
to. But twenty-four years of my livelihood—my
life—are in this store. I thought in ten years I'd
put it up for sale and retire. But as soon as people
see this is a changing neighborhood, they won't
touch this place. Or they don't want to give you
anything for it—they know you want out. I'd have
to take a tremendous loss if I sold it. But they'll
push me out. Maybe six months, maybe a year.
Another incident like this, I may close up
tomorrow."

Or kill somebody: Joe Castelli can still see that
pistol, still hear that loud *click*. One night recently, he spotted a Negro man jamming a bottle
into his trousers. Ordinarily he would have grabbed the bottle back—nothing more. But this time,

in a sudden fury, he snatched up a fifth of Christian Brothers by the neck and in a flash was behind the thief, ready to bring the bottle crashing down on his head. He felt DeAngelo's fingers close around his wrist. "I wanted to kill him," he says now. "Fred stopped me." Another night, a black man in a fur coat came in and stood briefly with his back to the counter. "He was reaching into the coat—he had his hand in there and he was turning around. I had the gun out. If anything had flashed metal I would have shot him." Castelli paused. "You know what he had? A little puppy. He had a puppy in there." He sighed heavily, in wonder at what is becoming of him and his world. "A puppy," he said. "I might have shot him."

3. The Cops

The evening was clear and mellow for August, a cool 67 degrees and breezy. Patrolman Joe Higgins nosed his unmarked squad car through the night places of the Gresham police district, watching the alleys and storefronts slide past, half-listening to the low staccato of the radio, exchanging shorthand grunts with his partner, Tom Cullen, slouched low in the seat beside him. They had been riding for three humdrum hours when, shortly after 9 P.M., they picked up the call: gunfire in the street up in the changing north reaches of the district. The two cops glanced at one another. Cullen got the mike out of the glove compartment and radioed: "Six-sixty is going in." Higgins hit the accelerator and snaked the black Chevy through the sluggish night traffic toward Shop-Rite Liquors—and the middle of his own neighborhood.

It was a different place when Higgins was born thirty-nine years ago—an all-white melting-pot mix of Irish, Italians, Germans, Swedes, and Poles in brick bungalows and two-family houses and occasional low-rise apartments. His father was a cop, a calling so common among the Gresham Irish that they called it simply "going on the job." Higgins never really thought of doing anything else: he came home from a Marine tour in Korea

16

with a Silver Star and, in 1955, went on the job, too. And, just as comfortably, he settled in the old neighborhood, in the brick two-family house where he lives today with his wife, three kids, and two dogs, and his widowed mother upstairs.

Now, however, the neighborhood has tipped 60 percent black, and it keeps on tipping every week. It is the all-too-familiar American urban rhythm: after the succession of immigrants come the blacks. But Gresham is a notch more complex. Its blacks came not from the cotton fields of Alabama and the tar-paper shacks of Georgia but down a few miles from the older, seething Englewood ghetto north of 63rd where the Black P Stone Nation rages and where dozens of black youths have been killed by gunfire in "gang bangs," the endless gang fights. After that, Gresham is a great improvement for the blacks. There are no real gangs, not much fighting, and the housing, while old, is much better. Nor has Gresham been crushed by the old-style panic-peddling of unscrupulous real estate promoters; much of that had died out by the time blacks began moving in a decade ago. The result is a neighborhood with more subtle problems. The houses are well-kept, the playgrounds and lawns are much as they were when Higgins was a boy. But there are changes that scream at *him*. As his car patrols Halsted Street, it rolls past a branch of the Chicago Public Library. A uniformed Chicago policeman can be seen through the big plate-glass windows, leaning against the stacks. "You never saw a policeman in a library a couple of years ago," he grumbles. "But if he wasn't there they wouldn't have any books left at the end of the evening." Up ahead is the old Capitol Theater, where he watched Laurel and Hardy movies. Now it is owned by Jesse Jackson's Operation Breadbasket. And with the changes has come a wash of ethnic tension and petty crime. In the old days, Higgins didn't have to worry unduly about his wife—"my bride"—working the midnight-to-seven shift as a registered nurse at Little Company of Mary Hospital. But he has caught three muggers on the block within sight of his place, and now at eleven-fifteen every night he pulls the unmarked car into an alley across the street and sits there in the dark until his "bride" is safely in the family Pontiac and off to her job.

Joe Higgins lives and patrols at that urban frontier where the dreams of the blacks and the memories of the whites collide, and it is a lonely and a painful place for a policeman. The big-city cop increasingly sees himself alone at the edge of a clearing, resented by poor blacks, looked down on by affluent whites, menaced by revolutionaries, hog-tied by courts and politicians. The sense of alienation is doubly keen on the Chicago force, which has modernized and professionalized itself enormously over a decade—and which saw much of the resultant goodwill collapse in the bitterness of the 1968 Democratic convention.

In the early 1960s, reformers preached that if police departments were only filled with better-paid, better-trained men using the latest in equipment, all the problems of crime and punishment would smooth themselves out. Chicago, with Orlando W. Wilson, former dean of the University of California School of Criminology, as its reform police superintendent, was following that logical prescription. Wilson streamlined the command structure and developed an innovative thrust that rolled on long after he retired in 1967. Chicago leads all cities in communications, with a remarkable system that can dispatch a squad anywhere in the city within thirty seconds of a telephoned call for help.

In a typical Chicago district such as Gresham—there are twenty-one in all—seventeen squad cars will be patrolling each eight-hour shift, along with four special "tactical units," three sergeants' cars roaming around, and two trucklike "squadrols," the modern version of the old paddy wagon. On top of that are all the traffic cars, under a separate command, the "area" units—homicide, robbery, burglary detectives—and the task force, a kind of mobile strategic reserve.

All of this is coordinated from one place—a well-lighted, quiet, temperature-controlled communications room on the third floor of the modern downtown headquarters. The city is divided into imaginary zones that correspond to telephone company circuits so that a call from any part of the city will automatically go to one of two policemen sitting in front of a detailed, lighted map of exactly that place. He takes the name, if given, and the location, writes it on a card, and hands it to another officer sitting beside him. With the punch of a button this man reaches the nearest squad and sends it on its way. In cases such as a chase, he can push a foot pedal that rings in every Chicago cop anywhere, including the traffic men and one of the two helicopters.

It is a quick, supple system. Many of the district stations are new, modern, low-slung buildings. Squad cars are new and generally clean and shiny. Since O. W. Wilson made it a point of honor a decade ago, one rarely sees an overweight or sloppy policeman. Uniforms are worn well. Shoes are shined. Policemen get to be sergeants and lieutenants because they can prove some knowledge of police work on tests, not because they know an alderman.

And yet in the riots and radicalism of the latter part of the decade, it turned out that professionalism and equipment weren't all that was needed for law and order. Psychic problems intruded. The Democratic convention of 1968 is becoming a dim memory for the nation's citizens. But for Chicago policemen it is a sour, ambiguous, lingering presence. At the time, Mayor Richard J. Daley had vigorously stated that yes, *some* Chicago policemen had overreacted, *some* Chicago policemen had been guilty of misconduct and should be weeded out, punished, and removed from the force.

Elaborate investigations ensued, and for the better part of a year the force was in constant chaos. Policemen were forever being called downtown either as defendants in civil service trials or as witnesses. Bearded, bell-bottomed photographers, reporters, and demonstrators paraded through, making accusations. But no policeman was convicted of anything and none was weeded out. At last check, every suspended Chicago policeman who wanted back on the force was there. They don't talk about it anymore. But they regard all the feverish hearings and trials as so much scapegoating. And they resent it. Then came racial tensions within the department, plus continuing rhetorical assaults by radicals.

Joe Higgins is an agreeable man, with spiky blond hair and just the beginning of a second chin and a paunch. He finds the present pass bewildering. Once, policing a peace demonstration, he asked a student dissident: "So what happens after you guys take over? You're going to have laws and you're going to have to have somebody to enforce them. So you're still going to need us." And the kid told him, "I never thought of that."

Higgins has plenty of time to think about it, riding the streets with Cullen as a plainclothes Tac Unit. The night-world sliding past his squadcar windows is in one sense changeless. "I figure," he says, "that there was crime before I came on the job, there is crime now, and there will be crime after I'm gone. It's been going on since Cain and Abel, and I don't think it's ever going to stop." But crime in the Gresham district is changing. There is more of it. It is getting younger, and blacker, and brassier, and unaccountably more violent. As a Tac Unit, Higgins and Cullen are expected to be experts in the particular kind of crime that goes on in their district: armed robbery and burglary. In rank, they are still patrolmen, but their long, unblemished records have earned them this special status. Never directly assigned to a call, they are free to roam in their unmarked Chevy all over the district, listening to calls on their zone radio and following hunches and that special intuition cops think they have.

Gresham is not particularly crime-ridden. The statistics kept downtown rank Gresham low among the city's police districts. Yet in the northern reaches, the changing part where Higgins lives, street crimes of some type occur on an average of three every two days. That translates into kids like Donald Payne sticking up liquor stores and taverns; purse snatchings and street muggings; theft from freight trains, often as they roll slowly through the yards; and burglary, especially the "roof jobs" where thieves—whom even the police consider professionals—cut a hole in the roof and let themselves in without disturbing burglar alarms. It all gets very operational—even clinical—to Higgins and Cullen. They cultivate long memories and patience. Sometimes they will shadow a youth they are convinced is a thief for months before catching him with the stuff.

Riding along in the dark, the little legends fly back and forth between them. There is Jerry, a black grade-schooler whom Higgins calls "an accomplished thief at thirteen." Jerry's thing was pilfering freight trains as they moved. Higgins has spotted Jerry and his friends in the act as he drove along below the high railroad embankment. "They break open the doors and pitch the stuff out, then come back later and pick it up." They can be foiled, he says, but not caught. "If you see them, all they do is swing off the train on the other side and run away." Once, Higgins says with a certain amount of glee, Jerry got angry at the low prices fences in the area were paying for stolen goods.

"He copped out on everybody. He told us everything." And Higgins and Cullen, nodding, agree with Jerry that the fences' prices were "just ridiculously low." "They'd give a kid twenty dollars for a color television set worth four hundred dollars," says Higgins in wonder.

Higgins and Cullen are students of criminal technique, and they think most robbers and thieves are incredibly inept. "You'd be surprised how many armed robbers use their own cars on jobs," says Higgins, "or cars they borrow from friends. They never wear masks, and they'll stick up a tavern where they've been drinking for years." The exceptions are the pros who pull the roof jobs, and Higgins seems in awe of them or, at least, of their skill. "These guys really make out," he says. "They know just what they want. They'll break in on a rainy Tuesday night—the best time —and just clean a place out."

But it is armed robbery that worries them most, because of the strong possibility of violence, a possibility they say is much greater than ten or twelve years ago. "It used to be," says Higgins, "that if you caught a stickup man and told him you were a police officer he'd put his hands up. Now they'll try to shoot you if they can." And they brood about the way ordinary people, shopkeepers like Joe Castelli, are buying guns. "Even though I'm a policeman," says Cullen, "if a man walks up to me and sticks a gun in my face, he's the boss. I've got a gun, but what good is it if I can't get to it? So these heroes who go for their guns, a lot of them wind up getting killed."

And it is coming closer to home. Higgins lives

just three blocks from Shop-Rite; he has traded there for twenty years, and when he saw Joe Castelli waving in the streets that August evening, he forgot about the shooting call and hit the brakes fast. Castelli blurted out the story and gave Higgins the license number of the black Ford. But it checked out to a fake address—a schoolyard— and Higgins and Cullen spent the next eight hours cruising the dark, fighting drowsiness and looking.

It was near first light when they spotted the car, parked in a deserted industrial area, with two black runaways, thirteen and seventeen years old, curled up asleep inside. The two patrolmen rousted the boys out, searched the car—and found the blue-steel .25 under a jacket in the front seat. The runaways, thoroughly scared, led them to a seventeen-year-old named James Robinson, who admitted having driven the car but not having gone into the store. Robinson led them to his kid cousin Frank, who admitted having gone into the store but not having handled the gun or clicked the trigger. And Frank Robinson led them to Donald Payne.

And so, red-eyed and bone-weary, Higgins and Cullen, along with a district sergeant and two robbery detectives, went to the little green-and-white frame house in Roseland at 9 A.M. and rapped at the door. Payne's sister let them in and pointed the way upstairs.

Payne was sleeping when the cops crowded into his little attic bedroom, and he came awake cool and mean. "Get moving," someone said. "You're under arrest." The police started rummaging through the room while Payne, jawing all the while, pulled on a pair of narrow-cut green pants and a full red jacket. "You don't have no warrant," he said. As Payne told it later, one of the cops replied, "We got a lawyer on our hands." But Higgins insists he misunderstood—"What I said was we'd *get* him a lawyer."

They marched him out past his family in handcuffs, took him to the district station, and shackled him to a chair while one of the officers started tapping out an arrest report: "PAYNE DONALD M/N [for male Negro] 18 4-19-52 . . ." Higgins got Castelli on the phone. "It's Joe," he said, "Come in—we think we've got the man." Castelli came in with DeAngelo. The cops put Payne into a little back showup room with a few black strays. Castelli picked him out—and that, for the cops, was enough. Payne was taken to the South Side branch police headquarters to be booked, then led before a magistrate who set bond at ten thousand dollars. The bounty is a paper figure: the Chicago courts require only 10 percent cash. But Payne didn't have it, and by noon he was on his way by police van to the Cook County jail.

Joe Higgins and Tom Cullen by then had worked ten hours overtime; in six hours more, Tac Unit 660 was due on patrol again. They talked a little about Donald Payne. "He had a head on him," Cullen said in some wonder. "Maybe if he didn't have a chip on his shoulder. Maybe—"

4. The Jail

He clambered down out of the van along with the day's catch and was marched through a tunnel into the white-tiled basement receiving area. He was questioned, lectured, classified, stripped, showered, photographed, fingerprinted, X-rayed for TB, blood-tested for VD, and handed a mimeographed sheet of "Rules of the Cook County Jail." (". . . You will not escape from this institution. . . . You will be safe while you are in this institution. . . .") He was marked down as a Blackstone Ranger over his objections—*I told them I was a little old to be gang-bangin'*—and assigned to a teen-age tier, E-4. He was issued a wristband, an ID card, and a celling ticket, led upstairs, and checked into a tiny four-by-eight cell with an open toilet, a double bunk, two sheets, a blanket, and a roommate. The door slammed shut, and Donald Payne—charged with, but still presumed innocent of, attempted robbery and attempted murder—began four and a half months behind bars waiting for his trial.

Jails have long been the scandal of American justice; nobody even knew how many there were until a recent federal census counted them—there are 4037—and found many of their 160,000 inmates locked into what one official called "less than human conditions of overcrowding and filth." And few big-city jails have had histories more doleful than Cook County's. The chunky gray fortress was thought rather a model when Chicago politician Anton Cermak opened it in 1927. He praised the "wonderful facilities of this building," and added the hopeful note that "not a single resident of the county of Cook will ever have to be incarcerated in it." Cermak couldn't have been more wrong, on both counts. The first warden hanged himself. By now, twenty-four hundred "residents of the county of Cook," about double the intended capacity, languish there. And the "wonderful facilities" have decayed through age, abuse, and lack of maintenance into one of the nation's most depressing jails. By the 1960s, the jail was run by an amiable patronage princeling named Jack Johnson. Ultimately, he was fired when a series of investigations found the jail ridden with drugs, whisky, and homosexual rape, and run by inmate bully-boys.

Johnson gave way to Warden (and now Director of Corrections) Winston Moore, forty-one, a round black Buddha with wounded eyes, short-shaven hair, a master's and a start on a doctorate in sociology, and some iron-handed notions about managing jails and jail inmates. Moore's mostly black reform administration has tamed the inmate tier bosses, cleaned up the cells and the prisoners, repainted the place for the first time ever, hired more guards at better pay, started some pioneering work and work-training programs, opened an oil-painting studio in the basement room where the county electric chair used to be, and begged free performances by B. B. King, Roberta Flack, Ramsey Lewis, and even, minus the nude scene, the Chicago company of *Hair*. But there has never been enough cash, and lately the John Howard Association, a citizens' watchdog group that gave Moore top marks for his first year, has turned on him with a series of reports charging a variety of cruelties within the walls. And worst of all is the desperate overcrowding. The rise in crime and the slowing processes of justice have flooded Moore's thirteen hundred claustrophobic cells with twenty-four hundred prisoners, most of them doubled up at such close quarters that if one wants to use the toilet the other has to climb on the bunk to let him by.

Roughly 85 percent of the inmates are black, and most, like Donald Payne, are stuck inside because they are too poor to make bail—not because they have been convicted of crimes. But the presumption of guilt infects the jail, as it does so much of the system of justice, and Moore squanders little sympathy on his charges. He grew up in black New Orleans, the son of a mailman struggling for decency, and when any of his inmates blames his troubles on hard times or bad conditions Moore explodes: "Bullshit! Don't give me that—I was there too, I know what it's like, and I made it. You got in trouble because you *wanted* to get in trouble."

The narrow eyes smolder. Moore confesses that he had one advantage a lot of street kids don't: "I had a father who would go upside my head if I got out of line. I fought kids every day to go to school. I figured I had a better chance with them than I would have with my father if I didn't go." He looked at the street kids with occasional pangs of envy—"They had the girls, they had the clothes, they had the money, they had the walks" —but he never joined them. And so today he has small pity for the Donald Paynes and enormous scorn for those white liberals who seem more concerned with explaining them than with punishing them. It is there that he sees the real racism of the system: "These bleeding liberals who have so much guilt that they can justify blacks killing blacks because we're immature. They're the ones who *keep* you immature. Quit justifying why I kill my buddies on Saturday night and try to stop me from doing it."

Moore has no such tender feelings: he provides rock concerts and painting classes but he also maintains The Hole—a tier of isolation cells into which the hard cases are thrown with no beds, no day-room privileges, no cigarettes, no candy bars, no visitors, nothing to do but lie or sit or squat on a blanket on the floor and wait for the days to go by. "You will always have to have a place like The Hole," Moore says without a hint of apology. "Much of the problem of crime is immaturity, and the greatest reflection of immaturity is rage—blind rage. There is no other way to contain it." The Hole nevertheless is a degrading place for people on both sides of the bars. The men crouch like caged animals, eyes glinting in the half-light. The guards in The Hole wear white because the men throw food at them and white is easier to launder.

It took Donald Payne less than twenty-four hours to get there. He came onto tier E-4 angry at being put with the gang kids and shortly ran into a youth from his block who had been a member of the Gangsters. "He had me classified as a Gangster too," Payne says. "He thought I was just scared to say so 'cause we were on a Blackstone tier. He ran up in my face and wanted to fight. We had a fight and I went to The Hole for thirty days and he got fifteen."

So they gave Payne a cage, and he sat it out. What do you do? "You sit on the toilet. You wait for the food to come around." What do you think about? "Gettin' out." How do you feel about The Hole leaving it? "It didn't matter much." Not enough, in any case, to keep him out: he went straight back in for four days for sassing a guard, emerged with a reputation as a troublemaker with a "quick attitude," and later did thirty more when Moore's men put down a noisy Blackstone hunger strike on E-4. After that, Payne was transferred to a men's tier and did a bit better. "Those Rangers," he says, "they keep talkin' about killin' up people. What they did when they was outside. What they gonna do when they get out." The older men by contrast idled away their time in the dayroom playing chess and cards and dominoes. They taught Payne chess and let him sit in. "People over here been playin' five and six years," he says, grinning a little. "They're pretty good, too. But I don't wanta be *that* good."

All the while, his case inched through the courts. Illinois requires that the state bring an accused man to trial within 120 days or turn him loose—a deadline that eases the worst of the courthouse delays and the jailhouse jam-ups that afflict other cities. But the average wait in jail still drags out to six or seven months, occasionally because the state asks for more time (it can get one sixty-day extension for good cause), more often because delay can be the best defense strategy in an overloaded system. Evidence goes stale; witnesses disappear or lose interest; cases pile up; prosecutors are tempted to bargain. "You could get twenty years on this thing," Constantine Xinos, the assistant public defender who drew Donald Payne, told him when they met. "Don't be in a hurry to go to trial." Waiting naturally comes easier to a man out on bail than to one behind bars, but Payne sat and waited.

5. The Court

The first time I walked into the Criminal Court Building, that odor hit me. That combination of sweat and onions and Polish sausage. I wanted to turn around and come out. I saw a guy I knew in law school and I said, "What is that smell?" And he said, "That's tears."

—Constantine Xinos, former assistant public
defender for Cook County, Ill.

It is a melancholy place, fly-specked and grimy, a Hollywood-Egyptian temple squatting heavily and incongruously among the factories, the freight yards, and the slum housing projects on Chicago's roiling West Side. Its out-of-the-way location is a monument to the failed business instinct of Anton Cermak, who dedicated the building on April Fool's Day, 1929, in hopes of sparking a real-estate boom in his home ward. The boom busted, and only the courthouse and its neighbor of convenience, the county jail, are left of Cermak's vision.

In its more than four decades, the Criminal Court Building has acquired a sad patina, grimy from the freight yards and grim from the endless wastage of lives. Some of the memories are merely banal. Others are too ugly to forget. Until it was moved to Joliet State Prison in the mid-1960's, for example, the court's adjoining county jail had its own electric chair. Executions came every few years and on the appointed night cars would be lined along 26th Street, the occupants out in the street staring at the old stone jail. At the moment the switch was thrown, always one minute past midnight, the power drain was such that streetlights would dim for an instant, telegraphing to the audience the moment of death.

Once, when crime reporting was very important to the flamboyantly competitive Chicago newspapers, the corridors were filled with colorful reporters. Ben Hecht's 1920s play, *The Front Page*, was set in the grand old high-ceilinged press room. Today that room has been converted into a courtroom. Reporters have to squeeze into a small, bare, first-floor room. The old routine court story has run away from them anyway. Once it was kinetic action. Minor hoods, booze runners, hitmen. Now the court is a collecting point for hundreds of forlorn, weary blacks, washed up on this dismal beachhead of society. It's not really a trial story anymore, it's urban sociology. But newspaper appetites being what they are, neither story gets told much.

The building has been altered, too, by violence within it. Last summer a black convict named Gene Lewis came to stand trial for his part in a prison incident in which an inmate was killed. Lewis already had one murder conviction, plus some local fame for several successful jail escapes. A girlfriend smuggled a pistol to him in court, concealed in a hollowed-out book. Lewis took a bailiff hostage and tried to escape in a judge's private elevator. But he never left the building. Police got him in crashing cross fire as he emerged from an empty courtroom. He died spraddle-legged in his own blood on the marble floor, eyes open, staring at the courtroom's big oak door.

They still talk about Gene Lewis. Bailiffs like to point to the spot where he fell. And in jail the prevailing view among inmates is that Lewis got what he wanted: he escaped from an otherwise no-exit life. "They gave him the chair," said one convict. "Then they brought him back down there again; they wanted to give him the chair again." And everyone who enters the building is hit with Lewis's legacy—a complete search in the outer lobby. Hand-scrawled cardboard signs tied to the brass outer doors separate men and women into two roped-off funnels where policemen and policewomen do the patting down.

Yet, for all its pathos, Criminal Court is just the very top of the pyramid of criminal justice in Cook County. The base is the enormous numbers of arrests made by police each year. The top represents the very small percentage of cases that actually come before the criminal court judges. Court officials estimate that in 1970 they processed about 4000 criminal indictments handed down by grand juries. To see how much winnowing out is done in the lower reaches of the system, match that against the estimated 400,000 non-traffic arrests made during the year.

Critics of the system point to this enormous reliance on the police—or input—end of the criminal justice system as one of the major things wrong with it. "What happened is that the police department is the only place that had any political sex appeal," says one criminologist. "The result is that the mouth of the vacuum cleaner is larger, the strength of the vacuum is stronger, but the bag remains as it was before."

What Donald Payne found when he got that far into the bag was a preliminary hearing in Criminal Court. On August 24, nineteen days after his arrest, he went from The Hole down to the basement tunnel, stripped naked for a search, then dressed and was led underground to the courthouse for a hearing in Room 402—Violence Court. Room 402 is a dismal, soot-streaked place, its business an unending bleak procession of men charged with robbery, rape, and murder, its scarred old pews crowded with cops, witnesses, wives, mothers, and girl friends jumbled uncomfortably together. Payne waited in the lockup until a clerk bellowed his name, then stood before Judge Hechinger in a ragged semicircle with his mother, the cops, the victims, an assistant state's attorney, and an assistant public defender and listened to the prosecution briefly rehearse the facts of the case.

Frank Robinson by then had been turned over to the juvenile authorities, and Hechinger dismissed the case against James for want of evidence that he had had anything to do with the holdup. But he ordered Payne held to the grand jury. The day in court lasted a matter of minutes; Payne was shuffled back through the lockup, the basement tunnel, the nude search, and into The Hole again.

On September 15, word came over that the grand jury had indicted him for "Attempt Armed Robbery (Gun) and Attempt Murder," and the case shortly thereafter was assigned to Circuit Judge Richard Fitzgerald for trial. And it was a package deal. With Fitzgerald, he also drew the two lawyers assigned to that court—assistant state's attorney Walter Parrish, the prosecutor, and Constantine P. Xinos, the public defender.

Criminal Court whirs along on three engines, each with decidedly different thrusts: the judges, the prosecutor's office, and the public defender. There are private criminal lawyers, men with reputations in Chicago like George Cotsirillos, Harry Bush, Eugene Pinchim, and Patrick Tuite. But they are really outsiders, an appendix to what is a three-legged stool. Two of the legs are long and strong—the judge's and the prosecutor's—and it's difficult to determine which, in Cook County, has the most political power. Cook County unified its court system in 1963, creating in the Circuit Court one of the largest systems in the nation. All courts—magistrates' courts in the suburbs, the old justice of the peace courts, police courts, divorce, civil—come under the single system.

The prosecutor's office is rich in political power, too. The holder of the four-year elective term has a political power base second only to that of the mayor of Chicago.

The third leg, by far the weakest, is the public

defender's office. Yet without it the stool of justice would fall over on its side.

But it was nearly winter before Payne reached Fitzgerald's courtroom. All that time the judge would be pumping out cases, Xinos would be dealing, and Parrish would be pushing. Donald Payne would be waiting some more. The rhythm and regularity of life inside crept into his blood. Connie Xinos, appalled by the surge in black crime, thinks it might help a little to put one of those tiny cells on display on a street corner in the middle of the ghetto as an object lesson. But, talking with Donald Payne, one begins to wonder about its power as a deterrent. Payne was irritated by the days he spent in court; nobody brings you lunch there. "I sort of got adjusted to jail," he says. "It seems like home now."

6. The Defender

Connie Xinos disliked Donald Payne from the beginning. They met in October in the prisoners' bullpen behind Judge Fitzgerald's courtroom, and all Xinos had to go on then was the police report and Payne's public-defender questionnaire—*All I know is I was arrested for attempt murder on August 4*—and that insinuating half-smile. *He did it*, Xinos thought; all of them except the scared children and the street-wise old pros swear they are innocent but you get a feeling. And that smile. *He's cocky*, Xinos thought. *A bad kid*. Xinos has been at it less than four years, but four years in the bullpens is a long time. He thinks Chicago is dying. And he thinks thousands of black street kids much like Donald Payne—his clients—are doing the killing.

Xinos is thirty, the son of a Greek cafeteria owner and a child of the white Chicago suburbs, a stumpy young bachelor with quizzical eyes, a shock of straight dark hair, and a Marine Reserve pin glinting gold in the lapel of his three-piece suit. He came to the building a year out of John Marshall Law School, hoping for a job as an assistant state's attorney ("It seemed glamorous— you don't get parking tickets and you carry a gun"), but hungry enough for steady pay and trial experience to settle for what he could get. The state's attorney had no openings, so he went upstairs to see public defender Gerald Getty. "Don't even pay me," he said. "Give me a dollar a year. I just want to work." Getty asked him to get a letter from a Democratic committeeman for form's sake—practically everyone in the building from janitor to judge has some such connection—and hired him shortly afterward for $9600 a year to start (it was $13,600 by the time he met Payne). Xinos arrived bubbling with ideals, like most of the young lawyers coming into the office, but a senior staffer on his way out took him aside and told him: "Six months in those bullpens and and you'll want out. You'll go practice probate law." And now Xinos figures he was right.

Ideals die young in a public defender's office. Chicago's is one of the oldest and best in the U.S.; it was organized in 1930, three decades before the Supreme Court asserted the right of the poor to counsel in any felony case, and its staff now numbers sixty-nine, mostly young and energetic lawyers. But they remain enormously overworked, partly because crime rates keep rising, partly because all the defendants' rights announced by the High Court in the 1960s have vastly increased and complicated their caseload. Xinos and his colleagues, squeezed in four desks to a cubicle, handle more than half of Cook County's yearly 3,700 criminal cases; their clients are 70 percent black and typically too poor either to hire private lawyers or to make bail pending trial. At any given time, says Xinos, "I got a hundred guys sitting up in County Jail wondering if Xinos is working on my case out there." And he knows the most he will be able to do for 90 percent of them is "cop them out"—plead them guilty—"and look for the best deal you can get."

That they are all nominally innocent under the law is little more than a technicality: Public and private defenders learn quickly to presume guilt in most cases and work from there. "I tell 'em I don't have to presume innocence," says Getty's beefy, tough-talking first assistant, Tom Cawley. "That's a legal principle but it doesn't have to operate in a lawyer's office." It stops operating when a rookie lawyer discovers that practically all his clients come in insisting that they didn't do it. "You can almost number the stories," says one of Xinos' colleagues, Ronald Himel. " 'I walked into the alley to urinate and I found the TV set.' 'Somebody gave me the tires.' Well, God forbid it should be true and I don't believe you. My first case out of law school, the guy told me he walked around the corner and found the TV set. So I put that on [in court]. The judge pushed his glasses down his nose, hunched up, and said, 'Fifty-two years I have been walking the streets and alleys of Chicago and I have never, ever found a TV set.' Then he got me in his chambers and said, 'Are you *crazy*?' I said, 'That's what he told me.' The judge said, 'And you *believed* that shit? You're goofier than he is!' "

Xinos learned fast. "For a while," he recalls, "I used to go out on North Clark Street"—a crime-infested section of storefronts and rooming houses north of the Loop—"and go up to these places and measure off rooms. People looked at me like I was nuts." So did judges, and after six months or so Xinos quit measuring off rooms like Perry Mason and started operating—"swinging"—inside the building. You learn its folkways. "It's our court," Xinos says. "It's like a family. Me, the prosecutors, the judges, we're all friends. I drink with the prosecutors. I give the judge a Christmas present. He gives me a Christmas present." And you learn technique. The evidence game. The little touches: "The defendant should smile a lot." The big disparities: which judge gives eighteen months for a wife murder and which one gives twenty to forty years. How to make time and the caseload work for you. "The last thing you want to do is rush to trial. You let the case ride. Everybody gets friendly. A case is continued ten or fifteen times, and nobody cares anymore. The victims don't care. Everybody just wants to get rid of the case." Then you can plead and deal for probation or short time. You swing.

And you get callouses. You discover early that a lot of crime is black and that the bulk of it—black crime against black victims—is taken considerably less seriously than crime by anybody, black or white, against white victims. "There's one kind of law for them," Xinos recalls being told by an old hand early on, "and another kind for us." It was a hard lesson—"I was very liberal when I first started"—but everything, even the working vocabulary of the building, confirmed it. You learn that a "nigger disorderly" means anything up to and including the murder of one black by another; you learn that a black man convicted of raping a black woman may well get off with the minimum sentence ("four to five years and everybody's happy") but a "zebra rape"—black on white—means certain big time. And, since the bulk of the rape and murder cases you handle are black against black, you learn to swing with the double standard, too.

Only, if you are Xinos, you begin to wonder. You spend your days defending black kids you suspect are guilty of violent crimes and your nights thinking that violence is taking over the city. "When I was a kid," says Xinos, "a guy would stick you up, take the money, and run. Now they'll *kill* you. It's just wild. These fucking kids will kill you." His fingers fidgeted at a note to himself, Scotch-taped to his desk lamp. "Just like this goddam Payne. They don't even wear masks. You think you could get a guy to wear a fucking mask. A ski mask, at least. But no. They go into places where they've been drinking for years, they hold up guys they know out on the street. It's the Wild West."

So Xinos took an apartment in the distant suburbs; he carries a gun because he is afraid even to stop with a flat on the Eisenhower Expressway without one; he talks like a cop about how the law isn't being enforced and how sentences are too light. "This city is dead," he says. "The Negroes are going to take over, and when they do it's like the worst guy in the office getting to be boss— they're going to screw us for a while. I don't want to live in a city full of Negroes." So he is thinking of going into private practice with an old pal in Florida, and in the meantime he spends his days dealing for light sentences for kids like

Donald Payne. He does this partly out of what is left of his ideals ("They should have to prove every case, get the witnesses, put it on"), partly because that happens to be what he does. "We got probation for some kids who got on a bus and stuck the people up. *Probation.* It's just like Jesse James. Well, they didn't get on my bus, so screw 'em."

And, like any commuter, he tries to leave it all at the office. The ones you can't are the few you plead guilty when you really believe they are innocent. "When you're scared of losing. When they've got a case and you believe your guy but you lose your faith in the jury system. You get scared and he gets scared and you plead him." But the Donald Paynes—the great majority of his cases—are different. Xinos never liked Payne; Payne fought him and Xinos much prefers the pros who tell you, "Hey, public defender, I killed the fucker, now get me off." Xinos thought Payne should plead guilty and go for short time. But Payne clung to Standard Alibi Number Umpty-one ("I was home at the time this was supposed to have broke out") and demanded a trial, so Xinos gave him the best shot he could. He had to lay aside his misgivings—his upset at crime in the streets and his suspicion that Payne was part of it. "Me letting ten or twenty guys out on the street isn't going to change that," he says. "This violence—it's like Niagara Falls. You can't stop it."

7. The Prosecutor

The black kids over in County Jail call him "The Devil," and prosecutor Walter Parrish likes that. "They know I'm not afraid to go to trial," he says, smiling. He fancies that the edgy hostility he saw in Donald Payne's eyes was a tribute to his own hard-guy reputation. Yet there is nothing particularly fearsome about his appearance or manner. Parrish is a slim black man of forty-one, with close-cropped hair and a friendly, open face. He smiles a lot. His three-piece, Ivy-cut suits are in muted colors and he wears white shirts with narrow dark ties. He is playing by The Man's rules and he is making it.

Parrish knows about violence more intimately than does Connie Xinos. He did, after all, grow up in a ghetto. But he let it flow around him then and he does to this day, still layered with the defenses he needed to survive. Working in the bullpen every day, he sees the same things Xinos sees. But they have arrived there from such different directions that the same passions do not ignite within Parrish. He does think about it. But not too deeply. Asked how it feels to see all these black people riding the justice treadmill, he responds slowly and only partially, never really grabbing the issue. "Yes, what people see here in the building, with all the black people, it would seem that the world is going to hell." Then he pauses, searching. "Gangs have been going on in Chicago since I grew up. What is new is the willingness to kill. What we call the senseless killings." His voice trails off until he finds the textbook answers. "Here in the state's attorney's office," he says, confidence returning, "you are working for the people. There is duty. You have a duty to all the people."

He was raised on Chicago's West Side, traditionally the toughest ghetto. Now he has moved to the far south end of the city, out of the ghetto, into an area of well-kept apartments where middle-class blacks live and where he and his wife are raising three daughters. A law degree from Howard University, the right political connections in Chicago, and, for the past six years, his job as an assistant state's attorney have bought him this way of life and he grasps it all tenaciously.

It did not really come easy. He got his undergraduate degree at Howard, too. But it took time, what with dropping out for a semester here and there to work. Out of law school, he tried for three years to get a private law practice going in Chicago but he made little headway. He eased into the 24th ward regular Democratic organization, became a precinct captain, and got to know the alderman, George Collins, a burly, very dark black man who later went to Congress. He did some legal work for the organization and then, with Collins as his sponsor, signed on with the state's attorney at seven thousand dollars a year. At first he thought of it only as apprenticeship for the private practice he still dreamed about. But he has stayed, now makes eighteen thousand dollars a year, has a young trial assistant, and seems quite comfortable in his niche. Occasionally he talks about that private practice ("I would know all the tricks"), but he just as quickly argues against his own yearnings, figuring that overhead would eat into his profits so much he'd have to gross fifty thousand dollars a year to make what he does now.

He also enjoys the resources he commands as a prosecutor. Investigators? The state's attorney has ninety-three to the public defender's six. Police, the sheriff, the FBI? "All you got to do is call them." Pathology? Microanalysis? "Just pick up the phone. You've got everything at your beck and call." Parrish has even flown witnesses back to Chicago from Puerto Rico. There is a solid feel about being part of the state's attorney's office. It fills the entire second floor of the Criminal Court Building and has outposts on other floors. There is a vast, musty library at one end, a library that Parrish proudly asserts is the best of its kind in the state. There is a huge suite of offices for the investigators. Everything is crisp and neat. The assistants work two to an office, instead of being jammed in four and five deep as the assistant public defenders are. It is all stamped with the mark of efficiency. Through the double doors from the corridor is a high blond-wood desk and the reception area is all fenced off. Behind the desk, twenty-four hours a day, sits a Chicago policeman in street clothes. There are also assistant prosecutors stationed in offices just off the main room round the clock, ready to speed out in police cars to the scenes of important crimes. The state wants to start prosecution at the earliest possible moment.

Then there is the pungency of political power. Unlike Xinos, Parrish does not get parking tickets. But there is much more to it than that. Being part of the political organization in Cook County is like belonging to a very exclusive club. Or, perhaps, more accurately, it is like being a member of the family that owns the mill in a company town. And, given the scarcity of blacks who are willing to put up with it, Walter Parrish can not only look forward to an endless career where he is, he even could conceivably rise, in time. Perhaps all the way to judge.

The system is also a white man's world. Parrish is one of just six blacks on the state's attorney's staff and the public defender doesn't have any. Conventional wisdom would seem to say a defendant like Donald Payne would relish having a black prosecutor. Or that he would resent a white defense lawyer like Xinos. (Perhaps if he could known Xinos's inner thoughts, he would.) But it doesn't work that way, at least not yet. Courthouse regulars talk about a "certain growing militancy" in which some blacks insist on having black lawyers and so forth. But the ordinary ghetto youth arrested and charged seems to realize he is in Mr. Charlie's game. They see only a sea of white faces in court. "Color seems pretty immaterial when you're locked up," says the public defender's Tom Cawley. "All they want is to get out, and if a black lawyer or white, a black judge or white, can do it, that's all they want."

And Walter Parrish, the ghetto behind him, smiles that slow smile and says, "I let the defendants know I'm ready, that I like to go to trial."

8. The Judge

Richard Fitzgerald is one of the better judges in the vast Cook County Circuit Court system. The Chicago Bar Association rates him well, and so does the shadowy world of gossip in the Criminal Courts Building. Prosecutors and defense lawyers alike regard him as "good on the law." They tell each other he is fair. It even seeps down the elevator, through the tunnel, and into Cook County Jail, where the accused consider themselves experts on judges.

"Fitzgerald is the grand old man of the building," says Xinos, whom the judge calls "Connie" from the bench. "Fitz is the best judge for law, the fairest. He's like God. He looks like God would look, he acts like God would act if God were a judge. He doesn't take any shit."

He is a handsome fifty-seven, with a ruddy, pink-tinged Irish face rimmed in silver hair that crawls down his neck to a point perilously near his shirt collar. He talks in hearty bursts and his face is creased to smile. Yet in court, with his silken black robes and black-rimmed glasses, he is stern. His mouth settles down at the corners like tar melting in the sun. If he seems like God to Xinos, so much more must he to the young black defendants who stand below him. The image must have seemed a closer reality of deity and ultimate judgment than anything Donald Payne had encountered in his stepfather's storefront Missionary Baptist Church. Because for Payne, and all the other defendants, Fitzgerald made crucial decisions with their lives. The judge is the system's fulcrum. Lawyers balance on either side. And for the accused, he stands between freedom and prison, between here and there.

The judge is also clothed in isolation. It gives him a freer hand than anyone else in the chain of justice, with the possible exception of arresting officers. Like his fellow judges, Fitzgerald operates with little actual supervision or public notice. Once elected, even a good judge has only a narrow fame. Bar association reviews come only at voting time, and even the elections themselves do not bring much attention. Running for judge in Cook County is a particularly anonymous political act. You run unopposed on your record, with voters choosing only: yes, you may remain a judge, or no, you should not.

The sheer weight of so many names on the ballot, and the fact that nobody really knows what a judge's "record" is means voters never say no. A judge gets on the bench in the first place through the political system, and if he doesn't make waves the system will not bother him at all. "In our form of government," says the University of Chicago's Hans Mattick, "we protect the courts from undue influences from other branches of government. The result is that the courts constitute one of our last medieval fiefdoms."

The day-to-day life of Criminal Court is also effectively removed from public scrutiny. The building's off-the-beaten-track west side location means only those vitally involved—the justice operators, the accused and their families, and the witnesses—ever see it. The crush of cases limits press coverage. Each of Chicago's four daily newspapers station a reporter in the court building, as do the wire services and the City News Bureau of Chicago, a local news service. But that is only seven reporters at most. Each of the 17 judges funnels some five hundred indictments a year through his court, a rate of more than two a day. So only the most lurid cases—the spectacular murders, those involving prominent people—are covered. The result is that on most days Judge Fitzgerald's closest friends do not know what he is deciding. For his part, he likes it that way. He loathes the position of his counterpart in small towns. "In a place like that," he says, "where everybody knows what's going on, an armed robber might get thirty to forty years. The judge has to do it because he's got to walk down Main Street and talk to all the people in the town, and they'll know what he gave the guy." But not in Cook County. "We're immune to such pressures," Fitzgerald says. "The public couldn't care less whether a guy gets thirty years or probation." He believes this works in behalf of the accused. "They get better justice; we're much more concerned here with the defendant than with public pressure. When you get into a small town, everybody gets into the act."

Fitzgerald's path to the bench was neither sinister nor particularly lofty, but it shows how the political system functions. In 1960, when Chicago Mayor Richard J. Daley was still consolidating his power as boss of the Cook County Democratic organization, a challenge to the mayor developed in a primary election for governor. Fitzgerald had retired the year before as township Democratic committeeman in suburban Calumet City. His successor mounted a minor revolt to the Daley leadership, but Fitzgerald stayed with Daley. Four years later, when the doughty Chicago mayor was even more firmly in control, Fitzgerald got his reward—he was nominated for judge and elected.

A new judge among the horde, he did a short apprenticeship in Divorce Court, which he hated. "Jeez, I'd rather give a guy the chair than take five kids away from their mother," he says. Then he moved to Criminal Court, found the work exciting, and began building his reputation. He arrives at court just before 9 A.M. each day and is usually already seated behind his big desk when Walter Parrish and Connie Xinos stroll in to discuss the day's docket. A bailiff brings hot coffee and the three sit in the large, dark, starkly furnished office just behind the courtroom, locked in amiable but businesslike discussion.

Though not really a legal scholar, Fitzgerald has followed the shifts and contours of criminal law with great interest. Charting the Supreme Court decisions from the Warren court into the 1970s, he sees "tremendous safeguards" for defendants, "far greater than we ever intended when we adopted the first ten amendments." The accused, he feels, "are clothed in swaddling clothes and laid in a manger of bliss." Still, he thinks public fears that prisons would open like floodgates are grossly exaggerated. "These decisions focused attention on the laxity of police work. It's refined police work—compelling them to do a better job."

Fitzgerald says he has developed a "seventh sense, or maybe a sixth sense," about the possibilities of rehabilitation. But the linchpin, he thinks, is the length of sentence. It has to be just right. Too short and the man will laugh at the court. Too long could make him bitter. "These kids sometimes go down there feeling they got an awful screwing. They just go down and mark time whining, 'I'm going to get even with Whitey,' 'I'm going to get even with the pigs and society in general.' [But] if they feel the sentence isn't too out of line, they've got maybe a ray of hope." Fitzgerald is not sure just what makes a man a candidate for rehabilitation. "Some kids," he says, "are just antagonistic. They'll just sit in the cell. You could have nine Harvard professors down there and it wouldn't help." But up to five years, he believes, a man can still be brought back.

That's the mood he was in that winter day when Donald Payne came into his court. Up to five years. The outer limit.

9. The Trial

Everybody kept trying to talk him out of his trial. When they finally got to court, Xinos leaned across the defense table and whispered, "Plead guilty, asshole, you could get ten to twenty for this."

"Ain't no need for that," said Payne.

"You really want a jury?" Walter Parrish teased him. "Or you want to plead?"

"I want my trial," said Payne.

Everything in the building says cop out, make a deal, take the short time. "They ought to carve it in stone over the door," an old courthouse hand, then a prosecutor and now a judge, told a friend once. "NO CASE EVER COMES TO TRIAL HERE." The People vs. Donald Payne did, at least half way. But then his case went sour, and the deal got sweeter, and in the end Donald Payne copped out, too.

Practically everybody does: urban justice in America would quite simply collapse if even a major fraction of the suspects who now plead guilty should suddenly start demanding jury trials. The Payne case was only one of five hundred indictments on Judge Richard Fitzgerald's docket last year; it would have taken him four years to try them all. So 85 to 90 percent of them ended in plea bargaining—that backstairs haggling process by which pleas of guilty are bartered for reduced charges or shorter sentences or probation. "Plea bargaining used to be a nasty word," says Fitzgerald. Only lately have the bar and the courts begun to call it out of the closet and recognize it as not just a reality but a necessity of the system. "We're becoming a little more sophisticated about it," he continued. "We're saying, 'You're doing it, we know you're doing it, and you have to do it; this is the way it has to be done.'"

It all seems right to Fitzgerald and the other operators of the system. There is the efficiency of quick turnover of the daily docket, plus added discretion. They can manipulate men and prison sentences according to their own instincts, which they have grown to trust. Yet it all hinges on distortions in the present system of justice. The huge backlog gives judges a ready operational justification. And their sense of rightness comes directly from the enormous presumption of guilt hanging over everything. The accused have done *something*, so all we have to do is find the right punishment.

The engine that makes it go, the thing that causes accused men to play the game, is the cruel threat of big time. If ultimate punishments were relatively equal, a man would be a fool not to go to trial and try for acquittal. But the risks of trial are well-advertised. There is, for waiverers, the cautionary tale of one man who turned down one to three years on a deal—and got forty to eighty as an object lesson when a jury convicted him.

Still, Payne insisted, and Xinos painstakingly put a defense together. He opened with a pair of preliminary motions, one arguing that the pistol was inadmissible because the evidence tying it to Payne was hearsay, the other contending that the police should have offered Payne a lawyer at the lineup but didn't. The witnesses straggled in for a hearing on December 1. Xinos called Joe Castelli and Patrolman Cullen and, for a few monosyllabic moments, Payne himself. Had anyone advised him of his rights to a lawyer? "No." Or let him make a phone call? "No." But another of the arresting officers, Robert Krueger, said that Payne had been told his rights, and such swearing contests almost always are decided in favor of the police. Everybody admired Xinos's energy and craftsmanship. Nevertheless, Fitzgerald denied both motions and docketed the case for trial on December 14.

And so they all gathered that wintry Monday in Fitzgerald's sixth-floor courtroom, a great dim cave with marbled and oak-paneled walls, pitted linoleum floors, and judge, jury, lawyers, defendant, and gallery so widely separated that nobody could hear anything without microphones. Choosing a jury took two hours that day, and two the next morning. Parrish worked without a shopping list. "I know some lawyers say fat people are jolly and Germans are strict," he says, "but none of that's true in my experience. If you get twelve people who say they'll listen, you're all right." Xinos, however, is a hunch player. He got two blacks on the jury and was particularly pleased with one of them, a light-skinned Urban League woman who looked to him as if she might be sympathetic. And he deliberately let one hardhat sort on the panel, black defendant or no. Xinos had a point to make about the pistol—you couldn't click it more than once without pulling back the slide to cock it—and the hard-hat looked as if he knew guns.

That afternoon, with the dim, hard light of winter filtering through the dirty windows, the case began to unfold. The opening statements defined the opponents. Walter Parrish is slow and methodical, undramatic in the extreme. "The evidence will show," he began, in a friendly monotone, then marched through the facts in the legalese policemen and prosecutors favor. The story came out in paragraphs—the store, the victims, the "attempt robbery," the "attempt murder," each prefaced in monotonous cadence with the words, "The evidence will further show . . . ."

Xinos bounced to his feet and kept in constant motion. He was breezy, confident, brash. "What Mr. Parrish has indicated to you is not evidence," he began. ". . . it may be what he hopes to prove, but it is certainly not proof." Xinos talked about the presumption of innocence, how the defendant did not have to testify or do anything at all in his own behalf. He promised to alibi Donald, in Donald's own words.

"He is not required to testify. . . . you will hear it from the stand . . . on the night of this robbery . . . the defendant was either at his home or within ten doors from his home during the entire evening." Xinos didn't say it then, but Donald's mother was prepared to make that testimony. Then Xinos, talking rapidly, described how he would undermine Castelli's eyewitness account. The description "could fit a hundred to a thousand or ten thousand young Negroes in this city."

With Xinos back in his chair, Parrish slowly rose and, in his stiff way, began to put on his case. He opened with the victims, and Castelli laid the story on the record: "About ten after nine the gentleman walked in. . . . He had a small-caliber pistol. . . . I edged away. . . . the other lad came up to me and he said, 'Shoot him, shoot him, shoot him. . . . [The first youth] pointed the gun at me and fired three times or four—at least I heard three clicks."

And the gunman—did Castelli see him in court?

"Yes, I do, sir."

"And would you point him out, please?"

Castelli gestured toward the single table shared by the prosecution and defense. "That," he said, "is Donald Payne."

But Xinos, on cross-examination, picked skillfully at Parrish's case. Playing to his hardhat on the jury, he asked Castelli whether the stickup man had one or two hands on the gun. "Only one, sir," said Castelli. "And was that trigger pulled in rapid succession—click-click-click?" Xinos pressed. "Yes, sir," said Castelli, and Xinos had his point, it takes two hands to keep pulling the slide and clicking the trigger.

Next came the matter of Castelli's description. He had told Joe Higgins the night of the incident that the gunman weighed about 185 pounds, 30 more than Donald Payne carried on his spindly six-foot-one-inch frame. Payne had nearly botched that point by wearing a billowy, cape-shaped jacket to court, but Xinos got him—after considerable wrangling—to fold it up and sit on it so the jurors could see how bony he was.

But the witnesses were wary. They could see Donald's bony frame, too, and they became reluctant to recall describing Donald as heavier than he is. So Xinos had to dig. He put Castelli's clerk, Fred DeAngelo, under cross-examination. "Did you . . . give a description of either or both men to members of the Chicago Police Department?" asked Xinos.

"Yes, sir," said DeAngelo quietly.

"Do you recall at that time how tall you said the men were?"

"Approximately one was . . . my height and the other was shorter."

"And how tall are you, sir?"

"About six foot."

"How much do you weigh?"

"About 148 right now. I just got out of the hospital."

Xinos closed in. "Do you recall giving any other description . . . ?"

But DeAngelo kept weaving. "I would say all I would say one was shorter than the other, one was taller and one was shorter . . . . As I said, the one man was about my physical size."

As Parrish objected, and got overruled, Xinos kept pushing, but all he could get was DeAngelo's insistence that Payne was his size and he thought he had told the police that.

With Castelli on the stand, Xinos tried again. But Castelli's memory kept failing him.

"Do you recall now what you told the officers regarding the height and weight . . . ?" asked Xinos.

"I can't really say what I said right now. . . ." Castelli answered.

"Do you recall giving the police a weight which you thought the taller man weighed . . . ?"

"I don't think they asked me that. I really don't know."

Xinos whirled toward him. "Isn't it a fact that you told Officer Higgins and Officer Cullen at that time that the taller of the two men was 185 pounds?"

Parrish was on his feet, objecting, but Judge Fitzgerald quietly overruled him.

But Castelli held firm. "I can't recall right now. . . . One was short and one was tall. What else can I say?"

Xinos let it go, moving on to something else. But the game finally came to an end when stocky, stolid Joe Higgins eased himself into the witness chair. The police report did, after all, list Payne's estimated weight—as described to Higgins by Castelli—as 185 pounds. And when Xinos got the string far enough out, Higgins said in flat tones that, yes, Donald Payne had been described that way. The thirty-pound misunderstanding was finally before the jury, undercutting Castelli's identification of Payne—and suddenly the People and their lawyer, Walter Parrish, were in trouble.

Parrish didn't show it, but he decided he needed something more. And he knew where to go—the Robinson boys, the two cousins through whom police had tracked Payne. Parrish had hoped he wouldn't have to put them on the stand. "It was a risk," he said later. "They could have hurt us. They could have got up there and suddenly said Donald wasn't there." But he was behind. He needed Frank Robinson to place Donald in the store, James to connect him with the car and the pistol.

So that afternoon, with court adjourned for the day, he ordered up subpoenas for the Robinsons. "We know how to scramble," said his young assistant, Joe Poduska. "That's the name of the game."

The subpoenas were being typed when Connie Xinos happened into the state's attorney's office to socialize—*we're like a family*—and saw them in the typewriter. Xinos went cold. He had talked to the mother of one of the Robinsons; he knew their testimony could hurt. So, next morning, he headed first thing for Parrish's austere second-floor cubicle. Parrish wasn't there but the Robinsons were. "We're going to testify," they told Xinos, "and we're going to tell the truth."

Parrish came in, and Xinos took him aside. "Let's get rid of this case," he said.

"It's Christmas," Parrish said amiably. "I'm a reasonable man."

"What do you want?" Xinos asked.

"I was thinking about three to eight."

"One to five," said Xinos.

"You got it."

It's an absolute gift, Xinos thought, and he took it to Payne in the bullpen. "I can get you one to five," he said. Payne said no. Xinos thought fast. It was a dead-bang case—the kind Clarence Darrow couldn't pull out—and it was good for a big rattle, maybe ten to twenty years. Xinos went back downstairs, got the Robinsons, and sat them down with Payne in Fitzgerald's library.

"They rapped," he remembers, "and one of them said 'Donald—you mean you told them you weren't *there*? Donald.' I told him again I could get him one to five. They said, 'Maybe you ought to take it, Donald.' I said, 'You may get ten to twenty going on with the trial.' And he said, 'Well, even if I take the one to five, I'm not quilty.' That's when I knew he would go."

But would Fitzgerald buy it? Xinos was worried. "The judge is the judge," he told Payne while they waited. "He might give you three to eight. You better think about it."

But Fitzgerald agreed to talk, and the ritual began to unfold. Xinos led Payne to the bench and announced for the record that they wanted to discuss pleading—"Is that correct, Donald?" Payne mumbled, "Correct," and, while he went back to the lockup to wait, the lawyers followed the judge into chambers. A bailiff closed the door behind them.

Fitzgerald sat at his desk and pulled a four-by-six index card out of a box; he likes to keep his own notes. Parrish dropped into a deep, leathery sofa, his knees coming up almost to his chin. Xinos sat in one of the green guest chairs in a row along the wall. There were no outsiders, not even a court stenographer. The conference, not the courtroom, has become the real locus of big-city criminal justice, but its business is transacted off the record for maximum flexibility.

Fitzgerald scanned Parrish's prep sheet, outlining the state case. Xinos told him glumly about the Robinsons. "We look beat," he conceded.

"Walter," asked the judge, "what do you want?"

"I don't want to hurt the kid," Parrish said. "I talked to Connie, and we thought one to five."

They talked about Payne's record—his jobs, his family, his old burglary rap. "Two years probation," Xinos put in hopefully. "That's nothing."

Fitzgerald pondered it all. He had no probation report—there isn't time or manpower enough to do them except in major cases—and no psychological workup; sentencing in most American courts comes down to a matter of instinct. Fitzgerald's instincts told him one to five was a long enough time for Payne to serve—and a wide enough spread to encourage him to reform and get out early. "Up to five years," he feels, "that's the area of rehabilitation. Beyond five, I think they get saturated." So he made up his mind.

"Will he take it?" the judge asked Xinos.

"I'll go back and see," Xinos replied. He ducked out to the lockup and put the offer to Payne.

"Let's do it," Payne said. "Right now."

A light snow was falling when they brought him back into court, grinning slightly, walking his diddybop walk. A bailiff led him to a table below Fitzgerald's high bench. His mother slipped into place beside him. He spread his fingers out on the tabletop and looked at them. The judge led him through the prescribed catechism establishing that he understood what he was doing and that no one had forced him to do it. Payne's yeses were barely audible in the cavernous room.

The choice now was his, Fitzgerald told him. He

could go to the pen and cooperate and learn a trade and come out on parole in eleven months; or he could "go down there and do nothing at all and sit on your haunches . . . and you will probably be going [back] down there for twenty or thirty years." Payne brushed one hand across his eyes and studied the tabletop. "I'm giving you the first break you probably ever got in your life," the judge said ". . . The rest of it, Donald, is up to you. Do you understand that?"

"Yes," said Payne.

And then it was over. Fitzgerald called the jurors in and dismissed them. They knew nothing of the events that had buried Donald; they sat there for a moment looking stunned. Xinos slipped back to see them before they scattered. "But you were *ahead,*" one told him.

Payne's mother walked out to a pay phone, eyes wet and flashing. "They just pressed Donnie," she insisted, "until he said he did it."

Parrish packed up. "An hour, a day—even that's punishment," he said. "One to five is enough."

Joe Higgins went back to Tac Unit 660. "Donald," he said, "is a very lucky man."

Winston Moore heard about it in his office at the jail. "One to five?" he snorted. "Shit. That's no sentence for armed robbery."

Xinos went home to his apartment in the suburbs. "One to five," he said. "Fantastic. Payne *should* go to the penitentiary. He's a bad kid, he's better off there. He's dangerous. He'll be back."

And Payne was sulky sore. He shook hands with Xinos when the deal went down, but when Xinos told him later what the jurors had said—*you were ahead*—he felt cheated.

Xinos thrills to the contest and he likes to know how things were going no matter what the outcome. The jurors gave him the impression that, even if the Robinsons had testified, Xinos could have undermined the testimony and won anyway. To Xinos that was pleasant to hear. And he could not resist bragging a bit to Donald.

But Payne could not view the trial as just one more test of Xinos against Parrish. And the feisty lawyer's little tale of prowess only confused him, gave him the sinking feeling he had been taken.

A break, he thought? "The best break they could have given me was letting me go." But there was nothing for him to do just then but go brooding back to jail. Recollections of that process he may not have fully understood would haunt him through the long nights ahead. And a year later, sitting bitterly in Pontiac State Prison, he could say, "You don't have to be found guilty to *be* guilty, and you don't have to be guilty to do time."

10. Prison

"You can write to your lawyer, your preacher, and six other people," the sergeant was saying, "only remember—your letters are censured [sic], so watch what you say." No. 69569, born Donald Payne, sat in the front row in his gray prison coveralls, his body at a deep angle, legs pushed out front, his half-closed eyes idling over the chapel wall from the flag to the sunny Jaycee poster—GOOD MORNING WORLD. Nothing controversial about prison in your letters, the sergeant was saying. "Let's keep this personal, fellas. Your parents get a lot of this on TV." No sex either. "Let's keep this down to personal matters, fellas. We're not in a Sunday School class but let's keep our hands above the table." And no letters to any single girls if you're married. No doubletalk, no jive talk, no hep talk, no profanity. "And fellas— don't risk your mail privileges by breaking the rules." The sergeant's drawn face was pasty, almost the color of his starched stiff khakis, and it never changed expression. The brittle, country Illinois voice never rose or changed. "The more mail you get, the easier it will be for you. It gets depressing in here."

Donald Payne was "in here" at last. The Illinois

Department of Correction had him now, night and day, to do whatever it would. To influence him, to reach him, to correct him. He had been marched aboard a black sheriff's bus in Cook County by first light and shipped with sixteen other county jail inmates to the Joliet prison complex, an age-yellowed, 110-year-old stone fortress on the wide flat banks of the Des Plaines River forty miles southwest of Chicago. It was a colorless February day—gray sky, no snow, lifeless, weedy fields turned winter brown. The bus ground heavily across the narrow iron bridge, snaked up the pitted highway between the yellow walls, and stopped inside the gates on a stretch of gravel parking lot.

The point of entry for a newly minted Illinois convict is the Diagnostic Center, a yellowing castle with Victorian hints across the road from the main prison. If a prisoner has come from a small-town courtroom and a one-room jail, a sheriff's deputy will drive to the front door and press the buzzer. The door has a tall glass with beveled edges. Inside is an elegantly proportioned entry hall. Only the pale tan bars beyond jar the notion that this is some gracious old southern Illinois turn-of-the-century mansion. A prisoner entering through this hallway could get a feeling of serenity. Certainly of individualized attention.

But Donald Payne never saw it. He entered through a narrow, dingy back door. Like most prisoners in 1970, he came not from the country, but from Cook County—where the streets pour into the courts, into the jail, and finally into this black bus. He drew his number, and baggy coveralls, and was stripped, showered, and shorn for six weeks of "diagnosing"—the testing, measuring, and probing of his baffling personality to determine which prison he would fit into best and what, if anything, it could do for him.

With his coveralls, Payne acquired a green cardboard folder into which would be slipped everything of importance about his life—his parole folder. It would proceed him three months hence to the parole board filled with far more information than Judge Fitzgerald and Walter Parrish and Constantine Xinos had when they talked out Donald's negotiated sentence. It would have a lot of his words, spoken to prison officials, some solid data from tests, a certain amount of professional conjecture.

For the testing, Payne committed no more of himself than he ever had back in Chicago's public schools. Coveralls aren't much, but Payne, sharp, flipped the collar rakishly up in back and left the front unbuttoned halfway down his chest. Cool. The testing was done in small classroomlike rooms. The men sat on wooden chairs with extended armrest-style desks. Payne sprawled in his. Each time the trusted prisoner administering the tests stepped from the room, Payne simply dropped his pencil. When the psychologist graded it, he found Payne had completed the first few pages and the last. Though Payne later asked to take the tests again, what he had done was considered enough to make the proper judgments. His level of cooperation was marked down as "minimal" and the paper dropped into his parole folder.

From the testing rooms, Payne went to one of

the staff psychologists for "classification," an interview procedure in which he was thoroughly probed and then judged as to his rehabilitation potential. There is a standard opening question and Payne was asked it: "Why are you in prison?" The story came out in a burst of words, all containing the same theme. "The only way I could get out of it was to plead guilty for the one to five. . . . They could give me anything. . . . I was home sleeping at the time. . . . The public defender said the case was beat but he wanted me to cop out, I don't know why. . . . All they had was the gun and there were no fingerprints."

Illinois, which was not notably progressive in penology in earlier years, did pioneer in the diagnostic concept—a reception procedure that includes testing and classification. Though the staff is small (it has to rely on the few well-educated prisoners who come through to keep it manned) it is professional and has systematically improved the testing methods. Care is taken to make them as culturally "pure"—free of bias against a person raised in, say, a black ghetto—as possible. Still, for all that, the technique sometimes outruns the uses for it. "We still have very few alternatives," says Dr. Frank Lanou, chief psychologist. "We have very little we can actually do with the information."

The dominant tradition in American penology is that the walls be strong and tall. Illinois has of late joined the progressives, slowly shaking its prison system awake from centuries of strongwall thinking. Richard Ogilvie, elected governor in 1968, took a risky step for a politician and made prison reform one of his major programs. "There has been more movement in Illinois prisons in the last eighteen months under Ogilvie than I have seen anywhere in my life, which is thirty years in prison work all over the country," says Joseph Rowan of the John Howard Association, a professional prison reform group.

Ogilvie picked Peter Bensinger, thirty-five-year-old son of a wealthy and socially prominent Chicago family, to head the streamlined department. Bensinger is no professional, but he does bring to the job enormous administrative energy and executive skill. He has energized the professionals and in Illinois they praise him almost to a man. For wardens he reached far down into the ranks. John Twomey, thirty-three, son of a small-town Illinois sheriff who recalls serving meals to his father's prisoners is now warden of the state's biggest prison, Stateville. Herb Scott, at Joliet, is a forty-four-year-old black sociologist of impeccable qualifications. At Pontiac, a medium-security prison filled with young Chicago blacks, wide, earnest John Petrilli tries to keep the communications channels open by pushing his considerable girth around the yard and through the cell blocks every day. Guard's salaries have been boosted from $480 to $620 a month.

With his new wardens, Bensinger has moved in small ways to increase the humanity of prison life. There is now Sunday visiting, which is eminently helpful for the visitors but was never done before because it slightly inconveniences the prison staff. Twomey has ended the dehumanizing process of having prisoners called to the visiting room by number. "We've taken everything else from the man. If we take his name too, how can he possibly feel he is a worthwhile human?"

In the bigger things too, Bensinger has tried to move from the warehousing of men to preparing them for the day they get out, as 98 percent of them do. He is changing the emphasis from rural to urban. Like many systems, Illinois prisons have always been heavily agricultural. This may get prisoners out in the air, but it hardly prepares a young ghetto black for reentry into the society of Chicago's South Side. Until just a few years ago, the farming was done in the style of 1900, plowing by mule team and so forth. And while the demand for street-wise city kids who can drive tractors and run hay-baling machines is limited, where can a good mule skinner get a job?

For all the movement, Illinois has a long way to go. "Sure, we've moved fifty years ahead," says Herb Scott. "We're now up to about 1850." And 1850 dies hard. The prison schedule is still a rural early to bed, early to rise. Donald Payne, a child of the city and a man who doesn't have to hurry to get anywhere, is rousted from his cell at 6 A.M., fed breakfast at 7, lunch at 10, and dinner at 3. He's locked up again in his cell before the sun goes down, which in winter is about 5 P.M.

"The language of prison," says psychologist Lanou, "is a mixture of industrial and farm terminology." Men are not moved from one prison to another, they are shipped. Eating is a feed, everything is a line. Signs directing movement around the inside of the walls are not addressed to men, but to tickets. As a man moves from place to place he must have his ticket time stamped in and out. So a typical sign, say, at the library, would be, "All tickets must check in at the desk."

Another major problem remains money. "We have to face reality," says Twomey, "All around us we see communities voting down bond issues for their own schools, to educate their own kids. Are these people going to want to spend more money for prisons? For criminals? It hardly seems likely." Even in time of great public demand for crime fighting, few people can catch the vision of what prisons perhaps could be. In prison, the man convicted of crime is for a period of time under the total control of society. The unmotivated black kid can drop out of his ghetto high school. But he can't drop out of prison. Nobody knows what makes up the criminal mind. But, as Twomey insists, "There is a great deal we do know, but very little of it is being put into use." The trouble is that any program to motivate or develop the personality of a convict, even when clothed within the grim patina of traditional prison life, can appear to the American constituency as the coddling of criminals. "If you believe the purpose of prison is keeping a person locked up, then this system has worked superbly," says Twomey, "but if you think of it as changing the value structure of an individual, then it just hasn't worked at all." Twomey and the other young Illinois reformers want to open up the alternatives, alternatives in how a man spends his time in prison, and how he will use it after he leaves. Right now there are few. For Donald Payne, after all the sophisticated measuring, the major choice was which prison he should go to: the maximum security prison at Joliet or Stateville, or Pontiac.

The psychologists described him as having a "passive dependent" personality with "an absence of conventional norms and values." And they recommended "counseling be directed toward establishing norms and values in view of the subject's desire for the finer things of life without resorting to conventional employment." But how to do that? One solution was to order him shipped to Pontiac, with all the other kids.

As they sent him, along with his slowly filling green-backed parole dossier, the sociologists assigned Donald Payne his "rehabilitation classification." There are five grades: favorable, problematical, doubtful, guarded, and unfavorable. Donald was marked "problematical." Later, at his parole hearing, he would be bounced down to "doubtful." But that was later. Payne headed for Pontiac, and the youthful offenders, with misgivings.

He had wanted Stateville, to be with the older men as he had in Cook County Jail. He feared gang banging. What he found, instead, was something like home. There are eleven hundred prisoners at Pontiac, the average age is a little over nineteen, and 85 percent are black. When he walked through the gate he heard his name. "Hey, Donald, over here." He remembers a sense of being welcomed into a family. "There were guys I knew. I didn't know they were here. They were just around the 'hood and then they were gone. I figure I know five or six hundred guys in here. They took care of me when I first came in. When

I was in the fish (new prisoner) line the first couple of weeks my friends got me soap, cigarettes, stuff like that."

Pontiac prison has no walls at all, just two chainlink fences topped with fat rolls of concertina wire. The grassy, well-clipped courtyards fade into the fences and inmates can get glimpses of the flat corn-planted countryside. It was built almost a hundred years ago as a reformatory in what was then felt to be a wholesome country environment. The air is clean and there is much room for athletic fields and enough grass to soften the look of old stone buildings. The prison is not crowded. Though cells are a cramped six feet by ten feet, each man has his own. The old buildings have been refurbished and are kept clean and neat. Day rooms at the end of each gallery of cells have lounge chairs and televison.

John J. Petrilli, a round, fat man of forty with dark, close-cut hair and a broad, serious face, has been at Pontiac less than a year. He finds reform a slow, painful process. "It will take two or three years to get the monster in motion." But he is trying. He has eliminated censorship of outgoing mail, provides Koolade for the men when they come in from the yard on warm summer evenings, and allows all kinds of expressions of individuality in cells. There are posters of Eldridge Cleaver and *Playboy* bunnies. He permits "any kind of books, except screwing for screwing's sake" and "all the black writers."

Most important, Petrilli has tried to cut down cell time—which is the idle time where men brood—and to get the inmates more involved in running the prison. When he took over he called all the men together and made a little speech. "I told them they should have pride in their institution. Their first reaction was, 'This is a fucking *jail*.' I told them they were here, I couldn't control that. But we could make it better inside."

He set up the Better Relations Committee, an inmate group with which he meets regularly. They gave him an early tip on a race relations program. He planned to start with orientation for the men coming in. "But they told me that first we had to tell those who are already here what time it is." The black city kids and the small town whites get along reasonably well, mainly because the blacks, who dominate, understand intuitively the community of interest. "We all brothers here," says Donald Payne, "everybody thinking about getting out. Ain't nobody going to jump on no white boy and maybe lose their chance to get to the [parole] board."

Still there is tension. The library's well-worn copy of *The Grapes of Wrath* bears this pencil-written exchange between two anonymous prisoners: "A lot of stupid rednecks. If you want to see how ignorant white people are, read this." And the reply, "If a nigger wrote the sentence at the top, you can see how ignorant the whole race is."

Petrilli rejects the authority style of prison control. He knows the risks, knows like all prison officials that inmates can take over a prison, take hostages any time they can get together. Still, he thinks the only real means of control is to convince men they have a stake in their prison, that both he, the warden, and the prisoners have to live together until somebody else decides they can go.

Wearing brightly striped shirts and wide ties, his jacket left behind on warm days, Petrilli, perspiring freely, endlessly prowls the yards and cell blocks, from the library to the vast clanking factory producing highway signs, to the dining room. The men stop him quite casually wherever he goes to unload their problems. He listens intently to each one, head slightly bent forward, face grave. He's moving as fast as money will permit into all kinds of programs—high school and college courses on TV, sports, a weight-lifting team. Yet he has few illusions. "A man is the sum of his experience. A prison can't control his environment on the outside." Neither, really, can it reach very deeply into a man.

Donald Payne has blended into the prison well enough. Petrilli finds him relatively trouble-free, though the warden and the guards do run up against that enigmatic aloofness, that opaque cask Payne has built around himself. Physically Donald finds things pleasant enough. "This is heaven compared to the county jail," he says. "This wouldn't be bad if I could come and go when I wanted." He has his friends. He catches for the baseball team. "I don't call this a penetentiary at all. Everything they got on the streets they got here."

And yet he has changed since those first days in court. His confusion over what happened to him seems to deepen by the day. His bitterness is translucent now, growing and alive. It squirms with fresh misunderstandings and the little indignities that arrive new every day. Early on he stood up in the dining room to get a spoon. He did not know that wasn't allowed and he spent three days in the prison "hole." He was disciplined by a sergeant for not tucking in his blankets. And another time he sassed the guard, whom he considers a "fool."

He broods. He thinks of the Robinson boys. He thinks of the judge. The prosecutor. Walter Parrish. Xinos. He was bitter at the start about Parrish. Now, as he plays over the whole scene in his mind in ever more confusing fashion, he extends his bitterness to the judge and Xinos. It all seems so conspiratorial, so collusive. "They jamming people. Xinos knew what the game was. I didn't need a lawyer." He rambles on that his arrest was illegal. That the police had no search warrant. "My mother and my sister would have testified for me. What other witness did I have besides myself?" Right after his trial he thought Judge Fitzgerald "fair." That has changed over time. "The judge has to give out a certain amount of time or he'll lose his job." He tells tales about the Cook County prosecutor, Edward V. Hanrahan. They could see him from the jail, pulling into the courtyard in his Fleetwood and walking, "grinning," into the building. "He goes in and jams some more people. Then they go out, have some coffee, have dinner. Then they come back the next day and jam some more." Most of all he broods about the Robinsons. "I lie in my cell and think about the Robinsons. They better stay out my way or there be trouble. I know I'm goin' stay out their way." He has heard that one of the Robinsons went to jail, the other to the hospital because of a drug overdose. He seems pleased.

Donald Payne has long had the habit of swinging his emotions rapidly in conversation without a change of voice or expression. Now, in prison, the swings are wider, more frightening. He swings so far in his bitterness there seem hints of violence. Then, suddenly, with only a flick of his eyes, he snaps back, to the farm in the forest, to the sweet life. He has kin in Greenville, Mississippi, and in Arkansas. He thinks he might stay with them. Or move back in with his parents, if they "move to a different 'hood." When he gets out he'll never come back again. And then, swinging again, he says he might. "You don't have to be found guilty to *be* guilty. You don't have to be guilty to do time. There's a lot of guys here didn't do what they're here for." He frets about life after prison. "I've thought about gettin' married. But people inside here get letters, say 'I'm pregnant' and they been in a year or two, or get divorce papers. And maybe I get out, get married, then maybe I take another fall. Then I guess I get my divorce papers in the mail."

As spring turned to summer in 1971, Payne began to look toward parole. His first shot at the board, by statute, would be July 6. He asked to be assigned to the prison farm, partly because the word inside is that the farm is a good place to avoid trouble, to do good time just before parole, and partly because of his fantasy about the farm in the forest. Petrilli was impressed with his sincerity, had him transferred. But Payne lasted only a few days. "He said the cows scared him," said one assistant warden.

As July neared, Payne worried about one rumor winging around the prison. "A lady predicted a riot in the prison on July 5," he says. "Fifty people will die. I could be out the next day. I don't care about that riot long as I get out."

11. The Parole Board

From the moment Judge Fitzgerald and the two lawyers agreed on Donald Payne's one to five sentence, his fate shifted from their more or less public hands to the invisibility of the Illinois Parole Board. To Connie Xinos, who tends to think in terms of early parole, it seemed Donald would be back on the streets by the next summer. He had already been in the county jail more than six months. Another six in prison and out he would come. Patrolmen Joe Higgins and Tom Cullen joked about watching out for Donald again soon. To Joe Castelli at Shop-Rite Liquors the thought was worrisome. He could still hear the click. Donald himself could not really believe in early release. Every time the subject came up with visitors he would pass quickly over the chance of early release and then say, as if to steel himself, "I may have to max it out," meaning until 1975.

The parole board, as it turned out, was just as pessimistic as Donald. Theodore Fields, the board chairman, sat in his spacious Chicago office and riffled through Payne's green folder. A Chicago lawyer and unsuccessful Republican office-seeker when Governor Ogilvie appointed him, Ted Fields smiles a lot, crinkling his eyes behind horn-rim glasses. But now, as he read Payne's file, he frowned. "This individual creates a very adverse reaction because anybody who has the capability of cold bloodedly pulling that trigger, under no stress, no danger, just because his companion yelled at him to shoot, we consider that a very serious thing." Fields looked up, stared at one of the many oil paintings produced by inmates that cover his office walls. "We are extremely sensitive to violence and potential violence. Now, when we see a boy like this who had this capacity within him, we're terribly alarmed."

Illinois now has a full-time ten-man Parole Board whose members rotate through the state's prisons a week at a time, conducting hearings, which are actually personal interviews, with each eligible inmate. Under Illinois code, a man becomes eligible when he completes his minimum sentence, and then each year after that. There are other factors—"bad" time and "good" time get folded into the equation to push the date back or forward—and every inmate burns the closest possible date into his brain. The board member who conducts the interview makes a recommendation to a "panel" of the board, which consists of at least three members. The panel breezes through the facts, considers the recommendation, and usually ratifies it.

The parole file contains the widest panorama of information on Donald Payne, the first time most of it has come together in one place. There is, on top, a summary of the accusation, trial, and results, prepared by the prosecutor's office. Then come police reports on the liquor store incident, his Chicago police arrest record which includes an incident of alleged rowdiness on a bus when he was fifteen which had been "adjusted" at the police station, a letter from the prosecutor advising against parole as a matter of course, a letter from Joe Castelli, all the diagnostic interviews and test results, full details on his previous probation violation, and various recommendations by staff people along the way.

Much of it, to the Parole Board's way of thinking, was negative. Pointing the gun at Castelli and pulling the trigger impressed every member of the board, from Ted Fields on down. Then there was the probation violation. Judge Fitzgerald had paid little attention to it, as had Walter Parrish. Even the police bothered little about it. Higgins, for one, wrote off the service station job as so much kid stuff. But to Ted Fields, "Probation is like parole. How a man performs on probation is a good indication of how he will do on parole. If he violates one, he'll probably violate the other."

The board pored over Payne's early arrest record too, though Fields was defensive about it. "People say you shouldn't consider arrests. But they are part of a man's total background." The letter from Joe Castelli was simple, emotional, and powerfully supportive of Ted Field's fears of violence. When the parole hearing nears, the board writes to the complaining witness asking for a reaction or comment. Castelli duly replied: "This man pulled the trigger three times. If the gun had gone off I would be dead instead of answering your letter. There is no rehabilitation for a person like this. . . . He should serve the full five years. . . . He will do the same thing. . . . Next time, someone will die."

And then there is the matter of his "institutional adjustment," how he gets along in prison.

The Illinois board, under Fields, tries not to put too much weight on "good institutional time." "A lot of people, including the inmates, think that's all we should consider," says Fields. "But how a man behaves in jail does not tell you necessarily how he'll do outside. But his previous record might be a hint." Even so, Payne's institutional adjustment would have impressed nobody. In June, about a month before his hearing, another prison sociologist reviewed his record for a progress report. Once again Payne proclaimed his innocence in an interview. The sociologist noted that "subject seems to experience little guilt." This time, the classification was changed from the earlier "problematical" to "no better than a doubtful prognosis." There was no riot on July 5, but the next day, when the hearing officer arrived at Pontiac, Payne was in the middle of five days of isolation for disciplinary purposes. To be called out of the hole for your board hearing is hardly an auspicious start. In conversation with the parole officer, Payne first said the charge should have been aggravated battery, not attempted murder. Then, in the next moment, he said he wasn't even there. Payne was sent back to isolation, the board member recommended against parole, and the panel upheld it.

Back in February, in his first days at the diagnostic center, Payne had told a visitor, "I'm starting my time now and I'm on my way home." But it's chancier than that. His time is a long and bleak one and, unless luck and will and the last chance processes of justice all work for him Donald Payne might be home right now.

Epilogue

The lesson of the People vs. Donald Payne and countless cases like it is that the American system of justice is less a system than a patchwork of process and improvisation, of Sisyphean labor and protean inner motives. Payne was arrested on chance and because of the tenacity of two policemen; he was jailed for want of money while financially better-off men accused of worse crimes went free on bail; he was convicted out of court and sentenced in a few minutes' bargaining among overworked men who hardly knew anything about him. It cannot be said that justice miscarried in the People vs. Payne, since the evidence suggests his guilt and the result was a penalty in some relation, however uneven, to the offense. But neither was justice wholly served—not if the end of justice is more than the rough one-to-one balancing of punishment with crime.

Because the punishment most commonly available is prison. And prisons in America have done far better at postponing crime than at preventing or deterring it. We have filled our jails with angry, confused men, most of them poor, most of them black. Undereducated by the ghetto schools they were peripherally exposed to, pummeled by the unnumbered forces in the cities of destruction, they sit in prison with time to deepen their bitterness and alienation. Donald Payne is not a particularly remarkable young man. His early years are duplicated by thousands of young blacks in hundreds of cities. But he and his faceless, nameless fellow inmates are a ticking time bomb buried deep in America. These are the men who together have triggered bloody riots, who represent the seed ground for growing revolutionary spirit.

The story of Donald Payne began as a *Newsweek* magazine investigative project. But it hardly ends with this chapter. Payne's future is exceedingly cloudy. And as long as his is, so is the future of justice and, further, the quality of life in America. Each of the steps in the process that buried Payne are full-blown problems in themselves: the growing petty but violent street crime that so baffles street-wise cops like Joe Higgins and Tom Cullen and sociologists and psychologists as well; the arrest and bail procedures that doom poor men to jail while rich men await trial in their own homes; the enormous assumption of guilt that pervades the criminal court of Cook County and its counterparts across the land and fuels the growing practice of plea bargaining; and finally the prisons and their woeful lacks. Each of these deserves the full glow of public exposure that responsible journalism can provide.

TRANSCRIPTS
OF COURT
PROCEEDINGS

STATE OF ILLINOIS } SS.
COUNTY OF COOK

IN THE CIRCUIT COURT OF COOK COUNTY
COUNTY DEPARTMENT—CRIMINAL DIVISION

THE PEOPLE OF THE
STATE OF ILLINOIS

vs

DONALD PAYNE

CHARGE:
Attempt Robbery, Etc.

REPORT OF PROCEEDINGS

JOSEPH X. TOURNIER, C.S.R.
NATHAN SHAPIRO, C.S.R.
OFFICIAL COURT REPORTERS
CRIMINAL DIVISION

INDEX

* * * * * * * * *

STATE OF ILLINOIS)
) SS
COUNTY OF C O O K)

IN THE CIRCUIT COURT OF COOK COUNTY
COUNTY DEPARTMENT—CRIMINAL DIVISION

THE PEOPLE OF THE)
STATE OF ILLINOIS)
)
    vs.   )
) Charge: Attempt
DONALD PAYNE   )   Robbery
                   Before the Honorable
                   Richard J. Fitzgerald

                   Tuesday, December 1,
                   1970, 1:15 P.M.

Court convened pursuant to recess.

APPEARANCES:

HON. EDWARD V. HANRAHAN,
State's Attorney of Cook County, by
  MR. WALTER PARRISH and
  MR. JOSEPH PODUSKA,
    Assistant State's Attorneys,
      on behalf of the People;

MR. GERALD W. GETTY,
Public Defender of Cook County, by
  MR. CONSTANTINE XINOS,
    Assistant Public Defender,
      on behalf of the Defendant.

THE CLERK: People of the State of Illinois versus Donald Payne.

MR. PARRISH: Mr. Payne is before the Court.

THE COURT: You may be seated until your lawyer gets here. We will proceed.

MR. XINOS: Sorry, Judge, I didn't know when you were starting.

THE COURT: I would like to know whether the defendant is going—I would like to know whether it is a bench trial or a jury trial.

MR. XINOS: Donald, what is your pleasure? Do you want a bench trial or do you want a jury trial?

THE DEFENDANT: Bench trial.

THE COURT: You realize that you have a right to a trial by jury, that is you have a right to have twelve people hear the evidence which the State presents, and they would determine your innocence or your guilt based on the evidence the State presents. Do you understand that?

THE DEFENDANT: Yes.

THE COURT: You have a right to waive that right to a trial by jury and have the Court determine your innocence or guilt based upon the evidence that the State will present. You understand that?

THE DEFENDANT: Yes.

THE COURT: It is your wish to waive a

trial by jury and have the matter heard
by the Court, is that right?

THE DEFENDANT: Yes.

THE COURT: You may make that fact known
by executing a jury waiver which I am
tendering to you at the present time.

MR. XINOS: Waiver is signed, Judge.

THE COURT: Very well. Let the record
show the defendant has executed a jury
waiver and tendered same to the Court.
Proceed.

MR. PARRISH: I understand there are two
motions pending, Judge.

THE COURT: I will proceed with the
motions first then proceed with the evidence on the case.

MR. XINOS: All right.

MR. PARRISH: If Your Honor please, our
witnesses are before the Court and open
court now at the convenience of the
defendant.

THE COURT: Proceed.

MR. XINOS: Which motion? Make any difference, Judge?

MR. PARRISH: Makes no difference to
the State.

MR. XINOS: Ready to proceed on the
motion to quash the arrest? All your
officers here?

MR. PARRISH: Yes sir.

MR. XINOS: We will proceed on the motion to suppress identification testimony
first, Judge.

THE COURT: Very well.

MR. XINOS: Move that all witnesses that
may testify in either motion be excluded.

THE COURT: All witnesses will be excluded until called upon to testify.

MR. PARRISH: Go with the bailiffs.

MR. XINOS: We have the arresting officer? Take the stand.

THE COURT: Swear the witness.

COURT CLERK: Hold up your right hand, please.

ROBERT KRUEGER,
called as a witness on behalf of the petitioner, having been duly sworn, was examined and testified as follows:

DIRECT EXAMINATION
BY MR. XINOS:

Q State your full name, sir, and spell your last name.

A Robert Krueger, K-R-U-E-G-E-R.

Q Where was your assignment on the fourth day and the fifth day of August, 1970?

A Area 2 Robbery.

Q Are you still a police officer with the city of Chicago?

A I am.

Q Did you affect the arrest of the defendant Donald Payne?

A I did.

Q Who was with you if anyone was with you at the time you affected that arrest?

A Officer Higgins and Officer Cullen of the 6th District, Officer Jackson of Area 2 Robbery, and myself.

Q Where was the defendant arrested? What location?

A In his home.

Q After—strike that. What time did you affect the arrest, Officer Krueger?

A This was at approximately I would say seven-thirty in the morning.

Q Did you know the defendant prior to that date?

A I did not.

Q Do you know if any of your fellow officers you were with at that time knew the defendant prior to that date?

A Not to my knowledge, no.

Q After you arrested Donald Payne, what if anything did you do with him? Where did you go?

A At the time of arrest he was advised of his constitutional rights and then taken into the 6th District.

Q Where exactly was he advised of and who advised him?

A He was advised that he had a right to a lawyer.

Q Did you give him these warnings or did someone else?

A I did not give them, no. My partner, Officer Jackson, gave them in my presence.

Q Please relate as close as you can remember what warnings were given to Donald Payne?

A He was advised that he had a right not to say anything, or anything that he did say would be or could be used against him at a later date, that he had a right to a lawyer, that if he didn't have the means to obtain a lawyer that the State would furnish one for him.

Q And on that same date, that is on August 5, and some time after the time that

he was arrested, did you or your fellow
officers have occasion to place this defendant in a lineup for showup?

A Yes, he was.

Q How many times was he placed in a
lineup for showup?

A Only once to my knowledge.

Q Remember, Detective Krueger, about
what time you conducted that exhibit?

A I didn't conduct this particular
lineup. It was conducted in the afternoon.

Q You were not present?

A No, I was not.

Q What time did your contact cease in
regard to this defendant on that day?

A At approximately nine hundred hours
that morning.

Q About nine o'clock that morning?

A Yes.

Q Between the time of the arrest and
the time your contact ceased did you hear
any officer in your presence advise Mr.
Payne of any other right which he might
have other than those which you just related to us? Understand the question?

A Other than his constitutional rights?

Q Other than the rights that you told
us that the other officer advised him of
in your presence, did you hear any other
rights or anything else pertaining to constitutional rights given to Donald Payne?

A No, I can't recall offhand.

Q You didn't give any more?

A I didn't give him any rights at all,
no, sir.

Q   The officer that gave those warnings,
his name again?

A   Is Officer Jackson.

Q   Is he here today?

A   No, he is not. He is on the medical.

Q   The other officers that were present
at the time of the arrest are they here
today?

A   I believe one of the other officers
are here.

Q   What is his name?

A   I couldn't tell you.

Q   He is in the back?

A   He is in the back room, yes.

Q   Do you know which officers conducted
the lineup?

A   There were two detectives from Area 2
Robbery from my unit that held it that
afternoon.

Q   Remember their names?

A   I believe it was James Tolls—not
Tolls, correction. It was Don Long or
Lawrence Stomp.

Q   Donald—

A   Donald Long or Lawrence Stomp.

Q   Any of those officers here today?

A   No, they are not.

MR. XINOS: No further questions.

CROSS-EXAMINATION
BY MR. PARRISH:

Q   In respect to Officer Jackson's illness do you know how long he has been on
medical?

A   He has been on the medical about two
months. He had an operation.

Q   Is he presently confined in a hospital?

A   Yes, he is.   I believe he is home convalescing now, but just gotten out of the hospital I believe about a week ago.

Q   Do you know what his condition was in respect to his illness?

A   Not really offhand.   I believe he had kidney trouble or something, and he had something removed.

Q   Is he movable?   That is the question.   To your knowledge?

A   Yes, I believe so.

MR. PARRISH: No further questions.

MR. XINOS: Nothing further.   Thank you.

(Witness excused.)

MR. XINOS: Mr. Sheriff, will you see whether or not Don Long or Stomp is in that back room?

Let the record reflect neither officer is here.   In that case I will call the defendant to the stand.   Mr. Clerk.

THE CLERK: Hold up your right hand, please.

DONALD PAYNE,

called as a witness on behalf of the petitioner, having been duly sworn, was examined and testified as follows:

DIRECT EXAMINATION
BY MR. XINOS:

Q   Donald, will you state your full name and spell your last name?

A   Donald Payne, P-A-Y-N-E.

Q   You are the defendant in this case, is that right?

A Right.

Q Remember the date on which you were arrested?

A August 5.

Q What year?

A 1970.

Q Do you remember what day of the week it was?

A Wednesday.

Q Remember about what time you first had contact with the officers on that day?

A I'd say it was about eight—about eight-forty-five, something like that.

Q Speak into the microphone as if you were talking into a telephone.

You say about eight-forty-five?

A Yes.

Q What were you doing when the officers —you first had contact with the officers?

A I was upstairs in my house asleep.

Q The officers show you a warrant of any kind?

A I asked them. He told me he didn't need a warrant.

MR. PARRISH: Judge, I ask that answer be stricken, not being responsive.

THE COURT: Sustained.

MR. XINOS: Q Was the officer who just testified, that is Detective Krueger, was he one of the officers that arrested you?

THE WITNESS: A Not to my knowledge.

Q Where did the arrest take place?

A In my house.

Q In your hourse? Where were you in your house?

A In bed upstairs asleep.

Q   What happened after you were arrested? Where were you taken?

A   87th and Green.

Q   What is there?

A   Police Station.

Q   While you were at the Police Station did you have occasion to be placed in a lineup or showup?

A   Yes.

Q   Do you know about what time you were so placed?

A   Two o'clock.

Q   Two o'clock when? In the afternoon?

A   P.M.

Q   Now, how many people were in this exhibition?

A   About five.

Q   Including yourself?

A   Yes.

Q   Did you have a lawyer at that time?

A   No.

Q   Up until that point had anyone advised you as to your constitutional rights regarding your rights at a lineup?

A   No.

Q   Did you at that time have any lawyer retained privately by you?

A   No.

Q   Up until that time were you permitted to make any phone calls?

A   No.

Q   How many lineups or exhibitions were you placed in on August 5 altogether?

A   One.

Q   Photograph taken of that lineup?

A   Yes.

Q   Did you at any time indicate to the

police from the time that you were
arrested up until the time you were placed
in that lineup that you did not want a
lawyer present?

A No.

Q While you were in the lineup?

A No.

MR. XINOS: Nothing further.

CROSS-EXAMINATION
BY MR. PARRISH:

Q In respect to the lineup, Mr. Payne,
was that lineup conducted in the same
room that you were physically brought into
after you were arrested?

A No.

Q It was conducted in a different room
other than the room you originally came
into upon your arrest?

A Yes.

Q You indicated, did you not, that no
one advised you as to your rights in a
lineup?

A Right.

Q Was there any conversation by any
officer with you in respect to your going
to a lineup?

A In respect to me going to a lineup?

Q That is the question.

A What you mean by asking me would I
like a lawyer, something like that?

Q No sir. From wherever you were when
you were brought into the police station
you went to another place to be put into a
lineup, is that correct?

A Correct.

Q Was there any conversation between the officers and yourself prior to the time that you went from one room to another to the lineup?

A Nothing but—

Q Was there a conversation, yes or no?

A No.

Q No officer said anything to you?

A Yes, they said something to me.

Q Well, before you got in the room for the lineup did you know where you were going?

A Not at the present time.

Q What time, if at all, did you realize where you were going?

A When I asked the officer.

Q There was conversation then, was there not, concerning the lineup?

A No.

Q There was no such conversation?

A When I asked them.

Q Is it your testimony, Mr. Payne, that you asked the officer whether or not he is going to put you in a lineup?

A Not the arresting officer.

Q Did you ask any police officer whether or not you were going to be placed in a lineup?

A The lockup officer.

Q You asked the lockup officer? What did he say?

A Told me two o'clock.

Q Was that before you were physically taken to the lineup or during the time you were going to the lineup that you had talked to the lockup keeper?

A Before.

Q   So you knew that you were going to be placed in a lineup, is that correct?

A   No, I asked.

Q   And he told you at 2 P.M., is that right?

A   Yes.

Q   Were the people in the lineup black persons?

A   Yes.

Q   Were they of the same build, similar height as yourself, approximately?

A   No.

Q   How tall was the tallest man in that lineup? If you can recall?

MR. XINOS: Objection, outside the scope of the testimony presented by the petitioner.

THE COURT: He may answer.

THE WITNESS: A   Say about three feet— about three inches over me.

MR. PARRISH: Q   About three inches over you?

A   Yes.

Q   How tall are you, sir?

A   Six-zero, six feet.

Q   How short was the shortest man you can recall?

A   Say about five-nine.

Q   All the persons were very close to being near your height, were they not?

A   I would say so.

Q   Were many of those persons in the lineup similarly built as you are?

A   No.

Q   Did you ask anyone when you came into the police station for a lawyer?

A   No.

Q Did you ask anyone after you came into the police station to see your parents or make a telephone call?

A No.

Q Did you tell anyone at the police station that you wanted a lawyer present at the lineup?

A No.

Q When you were arrested on August 5, 1970, were you told at that time what you were arrested for?

A No.

Q Did you ask the officer at that time anything concerning your arrest?

A Yes. Told me—

Q Did you ask the officer anything?

A Yes. I asked.

Q Did you ask the officers anything concerning why you were being placed under arrest?

A Yes.

Q Did he answer you?

A Yes.

Q Did he tell you you were being arrested for armed robbery?

A No.

Q What if anything did he say?

A Told me I was being arrested for murder.

Q Now, do you recall now what officer that was that made the arrest concerning you?

A It was a lieutenant or sergeant.

Q Do you recall his name?

A No, I don't.

Q How many officers were present at the time of your arrest?

A   About four or five.

Q   Were these officers in uniform?

A   The sergeant was.

Q   The sergeant was in uniform?

A   Yes.

Q   Do you recall his name?

A   No.

Q   You saw the officer that testified, Mr. Krueger, did you not, just testified earlier?

A   Yes.

Q   Was he one of the officers who came to your home August 5, 1970?

A   I don't think so.

Q   Were all of these officers who came to your home white officers or black officers?

A   Three white and one black or four white.

Q   Four white officers and one black officer?

A   Yes, or three, I didn't notice.

Q   Do you know their names of any of them?

A   No.

Q   Could you give a description of the sergeant that you said arrested you?

A   None other than he was tall and kind of slim.

Q   What about the other officers? Could you give a description of them?

A   One was heavy-set and one was light, heavy-set but rather short.

Q   Were these the same officers who took you to the police station and were these the same officers who conducted the lineup that you were in?

A Three of them took me to the police station. No, they wasn't.

Q These were different officers than the ones that conducted the lineup, were they?

A Yes.

Q Do you recall the names of the officers who conducted the lineup that you were in?

A No.

Q Do you know whether or not these officers were white or black?

A White.

MR. XINOS: Which?

MR. PARRISH: The ones who conducted the lineup. Q How many officers, if you know, conducted the lineup?

THE WITNESS: A About five or six.

Q There were five officers conducting the lineup?

A Other than the picture man, add him, about five or six.

Q Now, in the lineup that you were in, the only one that you were in, there was a picture taken of that lineup to your knowledge, is that correct?

A Yes.

MR. PARRISH: Thank you.

REDIRECT EXAMINATION
BY MR. XINOS:

Q Donald, while you were in that lineup were you nervous?

A No.

MR. PARRISH: Objection.

THE COURT: He may answer.

MR. XINOS: Q   When you were in that lineup did you have a piece of paper and pencil and write down the names of people that you were with?

THE WITNESS: A   No.

MR. PARRISH: Objection.

THE COURT: He may answer.

MR. XINOS: Q   When you were in that lineup, once you were brought into the room when the lineup occurred, how long did you stay in that room?

MR. PARRISH: Objection.

THE COURT: He may answer.

THE WITNESS: A   Approximately fifteen—

MR. XINOS: Q   Speak up.

A   Fifteen or twenty minutes.

Q   After the lineup was over where did you go?

A   Back to the lockup.

Q   Did you at any time while you were in that lineup have the occasion to go out into another room to see if there were witnesses out there or if there were people out there who had come to identify you, who they were talking to if anyone, if they were talking to anyone?

MR. PARRISH: Objection.

THE COURT: Sustained.

THE WITNESS: A   Just—

MR. PARRISH: Objection.

MR. XINOS: Just a minute.

Q   Was there anyone in your family or any—strike that.

MR. XINOS: Nothing further, Judge.

MR. PARRISH: The State has nothing further.

THE COURT: All right. Step down.

          (Witness excused.)

THE COURT: Take a verdict?

MR. PARRISH: Sure.

        (Interruption in proceedings.)

MR. XINOS: Your Honor, the petitioner rests.

MR. PARRISH: If the Court please, the respondent would rest on that motion.

        (Argument by Counsel, after which the Court ruled denying the motion to suppress identification.)

THE COURT: We will proceed on the motion to quash the arrest and suppress the evidence.

MR. XINOS: Yes, Judge. Again call Detective Krueger, please.

THE COURT: Swear the witness, Mr. Clerk.

        ROBERT KRUEGER,
called as a witness on behalf of the petitioner, having been duly sworn, was examined and testified as follows:

DIRECT EXAMINATION
BY MR. XINOS:

Q Detective Krueger, please, you are the same Detective Krueger that testified on the motion to suppress identification several minutes ago?

A I am.

Q Detective Krueger, when was your first contact with the case which is pending here, that is the robbery of Shop-Rite Liquors?

A The date and the time?

Q Yes sir.

A On the fifth of August at approximately, well, I got—we got assigned about
five-forty-five, got to the District
about six o'clock.

Q This robbery occurred the day before
on August 4 at about nine o'clock, is
that correct?

A That is correct.

Q You were not assigned to investigate
the original robbery?

A That is correct.

Q Up until the time you placed Donald
Payne under arrest did you talk with any
of the witnesses to this alleged crime
at Shop-Rite Liquors?

A Yes, I did.

Q Who have you talked with?

A I had talked to the victim, Mr.
Castellio.

Q Castelli?

A Castelli, yes sir.

Q Did you talk to anyone else?

A We had talked to another gentleman
who also had an encounter with the fellows
earlier that same evening.

Q Do you know that man's name?

A I would have to check with the
reports.

Q This is another person unconnected to
this robbery at Shop-Rite Liquors?

A That's right.

Q Did you receive any information
either from the victim of Shop-Rite
Liquors or from the victim of this other
offense which would identify Donald Payne

as the perpetrator of that offense
either by name, by nickname, address, or
anything else?

A Yes, we have.

Q From Mr. Castelli?

A No. There was—when we got assigned
this investigation the 6th District officers had in custody two young gentlemen
who they had arrested earlier that morning in an automobile that was used supposedly in this robbery.

Q When you say the automobile that was
used supposedly in this robbery, how do
you know that this automobile had any
connection with this robbery?

A Well, in talking to the victim he
stated that after the offender had left
his store a person came in and told him
that the fellows that just came out of his
store that they had observed them get
out of a Ford parked on the side street,
at which time he went over and seen the
car that was still parked there, obtained
the license number, and with this information he gave this to the officers. They
in turn in checking the area located the
automobile parked and there was two youths
sleeping in the car.

Q Hold on a second. Mr. Castelli did
not see the two robbers emerge from any
vehicle, did he?

A No, he did not.

MR. PARRISH: Objection.

MR. XINOS: Q This woman that gave the
information to Mr. Castelli and he gave
that information to you, do you know now
the identity of that person?

MR. PARRISH: Objection. That is a fact not an issue, who the person was gave Mr. Castelli.

THE COURT: We will hear it. He may answer.

MR. XINOS: Q Do you know the identity now of the person who allegedly saw two men leave that black Ford and go into Mr. Castelli's liquor store?

THE WITNESS: A No.

Q What time in the morning approximately was the automobile in question located, if you know?

A I have no idea.

Q Some time before six o'clock?

A It was before six o'clock.

Q Was this defendant found in that automobile?

A No, he was not.

Q Was anything that would tie the defendant by means of evidence to that automobile found in the automobile as far as you know?

A No.

Q Did you personally talk with the two people who were found in that automobile?

A Yes, I did.

Q Was this at the scene at which they were found in the automobile?

A This was in the 6th District.

Q Did you know these people prior to that date?

A No, I did not.

Q What were the ages of these two people found in the car?

A I would have to check. One was seventeen and the other one—

Q They were both teen-agers?

A They were both juveniles. One I believe was only thirteen years old.

Q Both Negroes?

A Both Negroes.

Q Both males?

A Males, yes, sir.

Q Did you at that time know whether these people, the juveniles, were reliable people so far as whatever information they gave you is concerned?

MR. PARRISH: Objection.

THE COURT: He may answer.

THE WITNESS: A Could you repeat the question?

MR. XINOS: Q You testified earlier that you didn't know these two people that were found in this car. When you questioned them despite the fact you didn't know their names, didn't know about their backgrounds, did you know anything else which would tend to make you believe or disbelieve these boys?

A No, I did not.

Q These boys were found with a gun, is that correct?

A There was a gun recovered on the front seat of the auto, yes.

Q Did you question these people?

A Yes, I did.

Q Did you get any information from them regarding Donald Payne?

A They related to me that they had met several boys and went into the automobile to sleep which was a practice of theirs. One boy was a runaway, and he had been sleeping the last couple of nights in the automobile during the evening.

Q After that conversation with them what if anything did you do insofar as anyone else might be concerned?

A We had—meaning myself—

Q Did you pick up anyone else based on their information?

A Yes, there were two other gentlemen picked up at that time and brought into the 6th District also.

Q Recall their names, officer?

A They were Jim Robinson and Cecil Robinson, two brothers.

Q Do you know the approximate age of those two brothers?

A One was eighteen and the other was twenty or twenty-one. He was an adult.

Q Did you know either of those two gentlemen prior to that evening? That morning?

A I did not.

Q How was it that you finally obtained information which led you to the home of Donald Payne?

A The one gentleman, Jim Robinson, was viewed along with other juveniles—the other adults and some other people in a showup, and at this time in the lineup the victim made identification as to Mr. Robinson as being the driver of the automobile.

Q Which Mr. Robinson was this?

A This was Jim Robinson. And in questioning him he told us that there was two other boys with him, one was Donald

Payne and the other one was a Frank
Robinson.

Q Up until the point where James
Robinson was identified in the lineup had
he made any statements regarding his complicity in any armed robbery?

A None.

Q Insofar as your information was concerned at that time, that is immediately
following that lineup when James Robinson
was identified, what did your investigation of this attempt armed robbery reveal
insofar as how many persons had perpetrated the crime?

A There were supposedly two perpetrators came into the business and one re-
maining out in an auto parked on a side
street.

Q After that lineup was it your belief
that it was James Robinson that had re-
mained outside in the auto?

A That is correct.

Q Following the lineup did you have
occasion to talk to either or both of
these two boys who had been found sleeping
in the car?

A Yes.

Q Isn't it a fact that upon talking to
them after the lineup that they confessed
to having committed the armed robbery and
attempt murder of Mr. Castelli in the
liquor store?

A No.

Q At the time you talked to these two
juveniles who had been found sleeping
in the car, that is when you talked to
them after the lineup was held, was

Detective or Officer J. Higgins present
and/or Officer T. Cullen?

A Yes, they were.

Q Did you learn from those officers on
that morning that these two juveniles
had confessed their part in the armed
robbery at Shop-Rite Liquors?

A No.

Q Did you present the information that
you had to a judge and attempt to secure
a warrant for the arrest of Donald Payne?

A No, we did not.

Q Were you persuaded at the time you
received the information from the two
juveniles and from Frank Robinson that
these three people were reliable people
upon whom you could—strike that—that they
were reliable people?

A Yes.

Q What was it that—what was it in your
brief encounter with these three people
that made them seem reliable to you?

A Well—

Q One boy was a runaway, right?

A Yes.

Q Was he the one that was sleeping in
the front or back seat of the car?

A I couldn't tell you.

Q There was a gun in the car, is that
correct?

A Yes, there was.

Q Both these boys were out after
curfew, is that correct?

A Yes, they were.

Q Find out whether these boys were at-
tending any school at that time or had
any employment?

A The one boy, I believe, was expelled
or suspended from school at the time.

Q What was it in your contact with
these three people that made you believe
that the information that they gave you
was reliable?

A In questioning, interviewing the two
youths in the 6th District after or prior
to the showup that they had not been involved in any robbery or any attempt
robbery, and in questioning them on how
long they had been in the car and who else
was in the car with them, what they had
done earlier that evening, they stated
that they were in the neighborhood and
that they had been sleeping in the car at
night and that when they come by the house
of the Robinsons they observed and talked
to the Jim Robinson, Frank, and Donald
Payne, at this time, and they left the
auto, and the two juveniles then got into
the auto to sleep for the evening.

Q How was it they came upon that gun?
How was it that gun was in the car? Did
you find out whose gun it was?

A The youth that was sleeping in the
front seat, I am not—I couldn't say which
one, when questioned about the gun
stated that he had no idea that the gun was
there and there was a coat laying on the
front seat that he had laid on top of,
and the gun was found under the coat.

Q Officer, that morning you placed a
man named Cecil Robinson under arrest too,
is that correct?

A No sir.

Q Do you know if he was placed under arrest by any other officers?

A Yes, he was.

Q Were you present?

A No, sir.

Q Do you know what caused Cecil Robinson to be placed under arrest?

A Cecil Robinson was in the home of Jim Robinson at the time Jim Robinson was placed under arrest.

Q What charge did you place Cecil Robinson under arrest for?

A He was taken into the 6th District for investigation or to be viewed in a lineup to ascertain if he was one of the perpetrators because he had fit the general description of the alleged perpetrator.

Q Do you remember the approximate description of Cecil Robinson in terms of age, height, weight?

A Cecil was a male Negro approximately twenty years old, six foot, 160, 170 pounds, dark complexion or medium dark.

Q When you went to the home of Donald Payne what if anything did you place him or did your fellow officers place him under arrest for? Exactly what time, if any?

A When we went to his home he was placed under arrest for the investigation of robbery, of an attempt robbery.

Q At that time was he arrested and charged with that robbery and attempt murder at that time?

A He was arrested and advised of his rights, his constitutional rights, and taken into the 6th District. Charges were not placed until after he was viewed by the victim.

Q   So far as you can recall when Donald Payne was taken into custody in his home up until the time that he was put in a lineup and identified was he charged with any crime up until the time he was identified?

A   No, he was not.

MR. XINOS: Nothing further.

CROSS-EXAMINATION
BY MR. PARRISH:

Q   Officer, in your conversation with James Robinson in respect to the person he implicated, Donald Payne, did he tell you where Donald Payne lived?

A   He didn't know the exact address but he knew the house and went along with us and pointed out the house.

Q   In other words, is it your opinion now as a result of his going along, his pointing out the house to you that Donald Payne resided in, that he knew where Donald Payne lived?

A   Yes.

Q   Did he give you the full and complete name of the defendant Donald Payne in his conversation with you when you asked him as to who was implicated along with him?

A   Yes.

Q   Did he tell you what time of the day or night that he first met Donald Payne on August 4, 1970?

A   I couldn't say.

Q Did he tell you under the circumstances which he met Donald Payne on
August 4, 1970?

A I can't recall.

Q Did he tell you the approximate age
of Donald Payne in your conversation with
him concerning who was implicated with
him in the robbery?

A Yes.

Q Did he describe to you Donald Payne
prior to your getting to the house where
Donald Payne was located?

A Yes.

Q When you went to that home—strike
that. Do you now know the address where
you arrested Donald Payne?

A I have it on report, yes.

Q Do you have those reports with you?

A Yes, I do.

Q Would those reports refresh your
recollection as to the address where you
arrested the defendant Donald Payne?

A Yes, it would.

Q Would you look at them, please?
Have you looked at your report?

A Yes, I have.

Q Has your recollection been refreshed?

A Yes. I do.

Q Do you now know what address it was
you arrested the defendant Donald Payne?

A Yes, I do.

Q What address is that?

A 4 South 100th Street.

Q That is in the city of Chicago?

A City of Chicago.

Q Now, when you arrested this defendant

Donald Payne was Frank Robinson present
at that time?

A He was out in the car with one of the
other officers.

Q In the police car, is that correct?

A Yes.

Q How many police cars arrived at the
address of 4 South 100th Street?

A Two.

Q Two police cars. And how many officers came to effectuate the arrest?

A Four.

Q Would you name those officers,
please?

A They were Officer Cullen, Officer
Higgins, Officer Jackson, and myself.

Q And also Frank Robinson was present
at that time in one of the vehicles, is
that correct?

A That is correct.

Q When you brought Donald Payne out to
carry him to the District Station was
Frank Robinson in the same vehicle or in
a different vehicle on the way back to
the District?

A Different.

Q Were there vehicles parked near each
other in the area of 323 West 104 Place?

A Yes, there were.

Q When the defendant Donald Payne came
out could he see into the vehicle that
Frank Robinson was seated in?

MR. XINOS: Object to that, Judge, I
think the physical—

THE COURT: Sustained.

MR. PARRISH: I will withdraw it.

Q In other words, Officer Krueger, the

information that was received, received
by you from Frank Robinson concerning
where Donald Payne resided, was in fact
true, was it not?

A Yes.

THE COURT: Excuse me. Is this Frank
Robinson or James?

MR. XINOS: There are two Robinsons involved.

MR. PARRISH: Q Frank Robinson is the
individual that gave you the information,
was he not?

THE WITNESS: A Yes, he is.

Q That information that he gave you
concerning where Donald Payne lived was in
fact true, is that correct?

A Yes, it was.

Q Based upon your conversation with the
complaining witness, Mr. Joseph Castelli,
concerning the physical description of
his assailants, in particular the person
that had the gun on August 4, 1970, in the
liquor store, did the information that
Frank Robinson gave you concerning Donald
Payne match substantially that description given by Joseph Castelli?

A Yes.

Q When you arrested the defendant
Donald Payne no gun of any nature or any
weapon of any nature was recovered in his
apartment or location, was it?

A No.

Q To the best of your knowledge—strike
that. You were not present at the
lineup, were you?

A No, I was not.

MR. PARRISH: Thank you.

REDIRECT EXAMINATION
BY MR. XINOS:

Q Detective Krueger, Mr. Castelli had indicated the weight of the taller of the robbers that came into the store was 185 pounds, is that correct?

A I have no idea.

Q Do you know if it is in your report?

A I don't have a copy of the original case report that was made out at the initial—only my own investigation.

Q Did you ever have occasion to estimate the weight of Mr. Payne in filling out any of your reports following the arrest?

A Yes, I did.

Q Approximately—well, what do you remember as being the weight that you attributed to Mr. Payne when you arrested him?

MR. PARRISH: Object to the form of the question unless it is established that this officer guessed at the weight and then put it in the box.

MR. XINOS: Q Did you at the time of making an arrest fill out an arrest slip upon which is contained space for the physical description of a person being arrested?

THE WITNESS: A I did.

Q Recall anything you put in a little box which is designated, "Height, Weight, Age"?

A Yes, I do.

Q Could you tell us now how you—what

you put in a little box that said
"Height"?

A Height as given to me by the defendant, because I had asked him what his
height was and his weight, and he gave
me six-foot-one, 157 pounds.

Q Did you have any reason at that time
to doubt whether that was Donald Payne's
height or weight?

A No, I did not.

Q Isn't it true that the weight which
was attributed to the robber by Mr.
Castelli was 185 pounds?

A I do not know what the original
weight was given.

Q How was it you were able to determine
that Donald Payne fit the description of
the man who was wanted for the armed robbery of Mr. Castelli if you didn't know
that original description?

A From the description given to me from
Frank Robinson, the youth involved.

Q He was merely giving you a description of Donald Payne, is that correct?

A That is correct.

Q Did you at that time know from either
your fellow police officers or from Mr.
Castelli or from the other victim who was
in that liquor store at the time of the
robbery the description of either of the
two robbers who had entered the store?

A It must have been given to me but I
don't recall. I am sorry.

Q Did you find any evidence in the
apartment—was it a house or an apartment?

A It was a house.

Q Was this the house where his family lives?

A Yes.

Q Did you find any gun anywhere in the house?

A We didn't make no search of the entire house.

Q Did you conduct a search in the bedroom?

A We got the boy, he got himself dressed, and we left. There was no real search per se made.

Q Did you find any weapons of any sort or anything which might connect Donald Payne with this armed robbery of Shop-Rite Liquors?

A None.

Q Mr. Payne resist arrest at that time?

A No.

Q Were you present when he inquired as to the reason for which he was being placed under arrest?

A Yes.

Q Do you recall if a response was given to him?

A Yes.

Q Do you recall who gave the response? Was it you?

A It could have been me or Jackson, I am not sure.

Q Remember what the response—how you responded to his question?

A He was being arrested for investigation of an attempted robbery.

MR. XINOS: Nothing further. Thank you.

MR. PARRISH: The State has nothing further.

MR. XINOS: Judge, I see from the police report which I am in possession of that Detective Higgins and Officer Cullen would be necessary witnesses. Are they here, Detective Krueger, do you know?

DETECTIVE KRUEGER: Cullen is here.

MR. XINOS: Cullen is here? Okay. Ask him to step out, please.

(Witness excused.)

THOMAS CULLEN, called as a witness on behalf of the petitioner, having been duly sworn, was examined and testified as follows:

DIRECT EXAMINATION
BY MR. XINOS:

Q Officer, state your first and last name and spell your last name, please.

A Thomas Cullen, C-U-L-L-E-N.

Q What is your profession or occupation?

A I am a Chicago Police Officer.

Q Were you a Chicago Police Officer on August 4 and August 5 of 1970?

A I was.

Q Who was your partner?

A Officer Joseph Higgins.

Q Were you assigned at any time on August 4 or August 5 to investigate an attempted robbery of Shop-Rite Liquors in the city of Chicago?

A Yes, I was assigned to make the preliminary investigation.

Q Do you recall the approximate time this attempt robbery occurred?

A   Approximately twenty-one-twenty hours.

Q   Be about nine-twenty in the evening?

A   That is correct.

Q   Of August 4?

A   Yes.

Q   When was your first contact with anyone who was involved in that attempt robbery?

A   About twenty-one-twenty hours.

Q   You were the original officers responding to the call?

A   Yes.

Q   In conjunction with that investigation to which you were assigned did you have occasion to make out police reports?

A   Yes.

Q   I show you what has been marked Defendant's Exhibit One for identification and ask you if you recognize it?

A   Yes.

Q   What does that purport to be, sir?

A   Robbery case report.

Q   Can you tell by looking at the report whether it was filled out by you or by someone else?

A   By me.

Q   You typed out that report?

A   Yes, I did.

Q   During the course of your investigation were you working with Detective Krueger?

A   Yes.

Q   Were you present at the time this defendant, Donald Payne, was placed under arrest in his home?

A　I was in the immediate vicinity.　I was not in his home.

Q　Did you drive to the address at which he lived?

A　Yes, I did.

Q　Detective, I call your attention to two juveniles who were arrested in this Ford automobile in which a weapon was recovered.　Remember that?

A　Yes, I do.

Q　Remember either or both of those boys being placed in a lineup after they were placed under arrest?

A　I don't recall.

Q　To the best of your information and best of your information in this investigation how many people were involved in this armed robbery—attempt armed robbery?

A　Three, I believe.

Q　That would be one person in the car and two people who entered the store, is that correct?

A　That is correct.

Q　Did you at any time believe that there were more than three people involved in this crime?

A　Yes.

Q　When was that?

A　At the time we found the automobile.

Q　Did you at that time believe that the two juveniles in the car were involved in the offense?

A　That is what I believed at the time, yes.

Q　You believed that the two juveniles were two of the three people that committed the offense, is that correct?

A Yes.

Q You didn't think that five people had committed the offense?

A Well, I didn't know how many people committed the offense.

Q To the best of your information at that time three people had committed the offense?

A Yes, that is correct.

Q Isn't it true that these two juveniles admitted being the ones who were responsible for this attempt murder and armed robbery of Mr. Castelli?

A I don't recall.

Q Well, calling your attention to this police report which has been identified as Defendant's Exhibit One for identification and ask you to look at the second page. If you have exhausted your recollection if you care to refresh your recollection by reading about one-and-one-half inches from the bottom of the typewritten portion.

I will ask you again. Recall—after reading this report does it refresh your recollection as to whether these two juveniles confessed as being the ones who perpetrated and attempted armed robbery and attempted murder of Mr. Castelli?

A They all admitted taking part in it after a showup.

Q Did you—when you say they all, that would be the two juveniles, is that correct?

A That is correct.

Q Did anyone else admit anything at that time? One of the Robinsons perhaps?

A   I don't recall if it was or not.

Q   At that time, that is when the two
juveniles admitted being part of the three
people that committed the armed robbery,
did you have occasion at that time to
believe that there might be even more than
three people who had perpetrated this
offense?

A   That is correct.

Q   What caused you to believe that there
might be more than three people?

A   Well, at the time of the arrest the
vehicle that they were in did not belong
to them. Was registered to a Mr.
Robinson.

Q   After you had arrested these two
juveniles two Mr. Robinsons were taken
into custody, is that correct?

A   Yes.

Q   One was Cecil Robinson, is that
correct?

A   That is correct.

Q   Who was the other one? James
Robinson?

A   James Robinson.

Q   At this lineup isn't it a fact Mr.
Castelli identified James Robinson as the
person who he had seen in that Ford
automobile?

A   That is correct. He identified him
as being the driver of the vehicle.

Q   So, Mr. Castelli had identified James
Robinson as being the driver and the two
juveniles admitted their complicity in
this attempt armed robbery, what was it
that caused you to believe more than three

people had been involved in the armed robbery?

A On information and interrogation of these boys.

Q Mr. Castelli see more than one person in that Ford automobile after it was being driven away by James Robinson?

A I don't know what Mr. Castelli saw in that automobile.

Q Did he ever indicate to you that there was more than one person in the Ford automobile as it was being driven away from his liquor store?

A I don't recall him saying anything about what he saw in the Ford automobile other than the driver.

Q Were charges placed against either of the two juveniles either on the adult level or at the Juvenile Court level?

A They were turned over to the youth division for proper disposition. That is Police Department procedure.

Q Do you recall whether they were charged with this attempt armed robbery and attempt murder of Mr. Castelli?

A No, I do not know what the procedure of the juvenile division is.

Q During the time—let me ask you something. When was it that these two juveniles admitted their part in this robbery? Was it before they were placed in the lineup or after they were placed in the lineup, if you recall?

A I believe it was after the showup.

Q What would you say, Officer, was the approximate time of that showup, roughly?

A About 7 A.M.

Q On the fifth of August?

A That is correct.

Q Recall whether Detective Krueger was present during the time of this lineup and during the questioning of the two juveniles which immediately followed that lineup?

A Yes, he was there.

Q Was he within hearing distance of the two juveniles when they were—when they admitted their complicity in this crime? As far as you can recall?

A I can't answer that. I don't know where—exactly where he was standing.

Q Do you know if he was in the same room?

A He was there.

Q Do you know if he was asking any questions of the juveniles?

A I don't know.

Q Do you know who was asking—remember now who was asking the juveniles questions? Was it yourself or one of your fellow officers?

A One of the fellow officers.

Q How many officers were in that room approximately during this questioning?

A Four of us.

Q You and Detective Krueger—

A And his partner, Detective Jackson I believe his name was, and my partner, Officer Higgins.

MR. XINOS: Nothing further. Thank you.

MR. PARRISH: The State has no questions.

THE COURT: Step down.

(Witness excused.)

MR. XINOS: Nothing further, Judge. The petitioner rests.

MR. PARRISH: May we proceed, Judge?

THE COURT: Proceed.

MR. PARRISH: Call Joseph Castelli, into court please.

JOSEPH CASTELLI,
called as a witness on behalf of the respondent, having been duly sworn, was examined and testified as follows:

DIRECT EXAMINATION
BY MR. PARRISH:

Q Would you state your full and complete name and speak loudly?

A Joseph Castelli.

Q Speak into the microphone.

THE COURT: Spell that last name.

MR. PARRISH: Q Spell your last name.

THE WITNESS: A C-A-S-T-E-L-L-I.

Q Mr. Castelli, on April 4, 1970, were you at or near a certain address in the city of Chicago?

A I was there on April 4, but the incident happened August 4. You said April.

Q August 4, August 4, I am sorry. On August 4, 1970, were you at the location?

A Yes, sir.

Q What is located at that particular address?

A It is a liquor store, sir.

Q Speak into the microphone.

A It is a liquor store, sir.

Q Who owns that liquor store?

A I do, sir.

Q Were you in that store at about
9:10 P.M. on that day?

A Yes, I was.

Q Who was in that store with you, if
anyone?

A Another employee called Fred
DeAngelo.

Q Fred DeAngelo?

A Yes.

Q Will you spell that for the court?

A D-E-A-N-G-E-L-O.

Q Were there any other persons in that
store at about that time, other than you
and your fellow employee?

A No, sir.

Q Shortly after that time what if anything occurred?

A Two young men walked in and one of
them held a gun in his hand.

Q Will you describe for the Court and
Counsel the description of that person
who you indicated held the gun on you
shortly after 9:10 P.M.?

MR. XINOS: Objection, Your Honor. The
question of probable cause depends not on
what Mr. Castelli—how Mr. Castelli de-
scribes him, but what was in the officer's
mind. Mr. Castelli wasn't present at the
time—

THE COURT: Might corroborate the report. Might be a way or means of corrob-
orating what the officer put in his
report.

MR. XINOS: The officer does not recall
even knowing the description given.

THE COURT: Sustained.

MR. PARRISH: Argue outside the presence

of the witness, Judge? I think it is proper.

THE COURT: Ask another question.

MR. PARRISH: Q How long, if at all, did these persons, the two of them that you mentioned, remain in this store in your presence?

MR. XINOS: Object again, irrelevant to the issue as to probable cause and to arrest.

THE COURT: If he connects it up.

THE WITNESS: A I would say a couple of minutes, two or three minutes.

MR. PARRISH: Q What did you do after these persons left your premises? Immediately?

A After he fired the gun at me I chased him outside of the store and I ran toward—they ran . . . and I ran after them, but I was unable to catch them.

Q Subsequent to that event you described did you have occasion to talk to someone outside of your premises in respect to a vehicle these persons allegedly arrived at your location in?

A A clerk from the store across the street said that somebody told them that they had come out of this Ford automobile, this black car.

MR. XINOS: Object. I know I went into it, but I object to the clerk from across the street saying who. If we can get an identification perhaps of someone's name.

MR. PARRISH: We be allowed to lay a foundation.

THE COURT: Lay a foundation.

MR. PARRISH: Q Tell the Court and Counsel that person's name, the clerk of the store, and what store he is employed at.

THE WITNESS: A He is employed at a liquor store directly across the street from my establishment. And the clerk said that the fellows came out of that particular car. So I walked to Paulina Street and I wrote the licenses down of the automobile and went back to my own place of business.

Q Did you have an occasion to call the police?

A Yes, the police were called immediately.

Q In respect to that license number that you had, did you turn that over to the members of the Chicago Police Department?

A Yes I did, sir.

Q Now, on the following day did you have occasion to view lineups or showups at a Chicago Police Department area headquarters?

A Yes, I did.

Q Do you know where you went to make that viewing?

A I went up to Gresham Police Station.

Q How many lineups if at all did you view?

A I saw two lineups.

Q And what time, if at all, was that first lineup conducted?

A The first one was roughly around five-thirty, six o'clock in the morning,

and the second one was at two in the
afternoon.

Q   In the first lineup that was conducted did you make an identification of
anyone?

A   The only identification I made at the
time was of the fellow that was in the
automobile, because he came into the store
and wanted to know why I took his license.

Q   Do you now know that person's name?

A   His name was Robinson.

Q   In the second lineup did you make
any identification?

A   Yes, I did.

Q   Do you now know the person's name you
identified in the second lineup?

A   Yes, Mr. Payne.

MR. PARRISH: Thank you.

CROSS-EXAMINATION
BY MR. XINOS:

Q   Mr. Castelli, this clerk from across
the street who you say works in the liquor
store across the street from your establishment, was it he who saw two men get
out of that Ford or was it someone else?

A   Someone else told him that they get
out of that car.

Q   This someone else, was this a man or
a woman, as far as you know?

A   As far as I know I couldn't give you
an account at the time. I don't know
which—or who it was, man or woman.

Q   Do you recall telling the police
officers who investigated this attempt
armed robbery of your store that an un-

known female entered your store and told you that two male Negroes had emerged from a certain black Ford?

A Right. I might have said that because I don't remember exactly. At the time I know that the clerk from the other store sent them over to tell us this, that they were, and this is when I went across the street and I took the license.

Q Your contact from across the street was this clerk from a liquor store?

A He told—they told us that.

Q Who is they?

A The people.

Q Take your time. I am not trying to confuse you. I just want to get it straight how you got the license.

A The clerk from across the street sent someone over to tell us they come out of that car. And I don't remember now, it was so fast, that I went just right over there and just grabbed the license number and came right back.

Q It wasn't actually the clerk that came over. He sent someone over.

A Sent someone over.

Q This might have been as far as you can recall a man or a woman?

A Right.

Q Whoever talked about that license number, bringing that information from the clerk, did that person talk to you or talk to your other employee?

A Talked to me.

Q Talked to you.

MR. XINOS: Thank you. Nothing further.

THE COURT: Do I understand it that the clerk sent somebody over?

THE WITNESS: A Yes, to tell me.

THE COURT: Was it that person who came over to see you had seen the people come out of the car?

THE WITNESS: A Come out of the car, sir.

MR. XINOS: Do that again, Judge.

THE COURT: It is my understanding his testimony the people who saw the people get out of the car told the clerk across the street. He in turn told those people to come over to see this man.

MR. XINOS: I don't read it that way. I think that the person who came over with the message merely brought the message and merely related what the clerk knew somehow. Is that right?

THE COURT: Is it my understanding that some people saw the two people get out of the car and they told the clerk across the street?

THE WITNESS: A Yes, sir.

THE COURT: He said, don't tell me, go across the street and tell you.

THE WITNESS: A Yes, sir. This is how I got the information.

THE COURT: And this person told him.

THE WITNESS: A Yes, sir.

MR. XINOS: Q The person who brought you the information, was it your impression that they had seen?

THE WITNESS: A This is what I gather. I didn't see them get out of the car.

Q What did this—

A I gathered what they told me they

sent them across the street. From across the street they sent them to my store to tell me that they had come out of this car, and I didn't question—I didn't question anybody, I just went over and got the license.

Q Let me ask you one question. The person who came across the street with this message, as near as you can recall what did he say or what did she say?

A Said that the party that were in the store, that run out of the store, came out of that automobile.

MR. XINOS: Okay. Thank you very much.

MR. PARRISH: No further questions, and respondent rests in rebuttal.

MR. XINOS: Have no further witnesses, Judge.

THE COURT: Thank you.

                (Witness excused.)

        (Thereupon the motion to quash the arrest and suppress the evidence was denied by the Court, after which said cause was continued to December 14, 1970.)

STATE OF ILLINOIS   )
) SS.
COUNTY OF C O O K   )

   IN THE CIRCUIT COURT OF COOK COUNTY
   COUNTY DEPARTMENT—CRIMINAL DIVISION

THE PEOPLE OF THE   )
STATE OF ILLINOIS   )
)
     vs.   )
) Charge: Attempt
DONALD PAYNE   )   Robbery, Etc.

REPORT OF PROCEEDINGS

   BE IT REMEMBERED that on the four-
teenth day of December, A.D. 1970, this
cause came on for trial before the Honor-
able RICHARD J. FITZGERALD, Judge of said
court, and a jury, upon the indictment
herein, the defendant having entered a
plea of not guilty.

   APPEARANCES:
     HON. EDWARD V. HANRAHAN,
          State's Attorney of Cook
          County, by
     MR. WALTER J. PARRISH and

MR. JOSEPH PODUSKA,
    Assistant State's Attorneys,
    appeared for the People;
MR. GERALD W. GETTY,
    Public Defender of Cook County,
    by
MR. CONSTANTINE P. XINOS,
    Assistant Public Defender,
    appeared for the Defendant.

THE CLERK: People of the State of Illinois versus Donald Payne.

THE COURT: Bring in the jury.

> (Thereupon the following proceedings were had within the presence and hearing of the prospective jurors.)

THE COURT: Ladies and gentlemen, you have been summoned here to my courtroom in relation to a certain criminal case in which an indictment has been returned by the Cook County Grand Jury charging the defendant, Donald Payne, with having committed the offense of attempt armed robbery in the first count and in the second count he is charged with attempt murder.

The defendant is represented by Mr. Connie Xinos, the gentleman seated at the right-hand side of the counsel table. The State is represented by Mr. Parrish and Mr. Poduska, the gentlemen seated at the far end of counsel table.

At this time, ladies and gentlemen, I will touch upon certain broad fundamentals relating to the trial of criminal cases in the county of Cook. My remarks at this time are in no manner intended to touch upon the law involved in the case. When we discuss the question of instructions to the jury preceding a trial, we are merely touching upon some of the broad fundamentals which you will be confronted with during the course of the trial of the case.

141

The instructions as we used them in the terminology of the Criminal Court have to do with the law which is embodied in the case. That law is in the form of written instructions which will be tendered to you at the conclusion of all of the evidence which you will apply to the facts and ultimately reach a verdict therefrom.

The indictment which the Court has referred to in the case is not to be considered as any evidence or any presumption of guilt of this defendant. The defendant under the law is presumed to be innocent of the charges contained in this indictment and that presumption of innocence remains with the defendant throughout the entire course of the trial.

The State has the obligation of proving the charges contained in this indictment beyond a reasonable doubt and that obligation remains with the State throughout the entire course of the proceedings.

The Judge is the judge of the law in the case. Now that law will be given to you in the instructions which I have heretofore referred to at the conclusion of all the evidence.

You as jurors will be the judge of the facts in the case. By that I mean the evidence which will be tendered to you from the various witnesses who will take the witness stand. Now it is within your province to give whatever weight you may determine you want to give to the testimony of the respective witnesses and you may accept or reject any of the testi-

mony that they give. However insofar as
the law is concerned in this case you are
obligated to follow the law that the Court
gives you in its instructions.

You may not like it, you may not agree
with it, but you must accept it and you
must apply it to the facts in this case
and thereafter ultimately reach your
verdict in this case. If at the conclusion of all of the evidence in this case
you are convinced that the State has
met its burden and has proven the charges
contained in the indictment and that the
defendant is guilty of the charges contained in this indictment beyond a reasonable doubt, then it would be your obligation to find the defendant guilty.

If, however, at the conclusion of all of
the evidence you find that the State has
failed to meet its burden and has failed
to prove the charges contained in this
indictment beyond a reasonable doubt, then
it would be your duty to find the defendant not guilty.

At times we will by necessity excuse the
jurors from time to time while we are in
the process of the general conduct of
other cases here in this courtroom. We
may be compelled to have a side bar conference with the respective counsel in
this case. You are not to assume that we
are in any manner trying to secrete or
keep any evidence from you, but these are
merely procedural matters which we follow
from time to time in the general conduct
of criminal cases.

Now in order to determine your qualifications to sit as jurors in this case,
you will be interrogated by the State and
also by Mr. Xinos representing the defendant. The questions that are pro-
pounded to you are certainly not in any
manner directed at trying to pry into any
of your personal background or any of
your personal affairs.

The general interrogation, the voir dire
examination which is conducted, is merely
done so for the purpose of obtaining
from your number twelve people who can act
as fair and impartial jurors. I am sure
that with the caliber of counsel that we
have before us you need have no fear as to
any questions that might prove embarrass-
ing to you.

From the twelve who will be selected to
serve as jurors in this case the Court
will admonish you from time to time not to
discuss the evidence that you have heard
from the witness stand either among yourselves, with any members of your family
or any of your friends or relatives, or
even the court attachés in attendance with
you during the course of the trial.

It is hoped that the ultimate verdict
that you would reach in this case would be
as a direct result of the evidence that
you hear from the witness stand, and ultimately through your deliberations you
will determine the innocence or the guilt
of this defendant.

We don't want any news media in any
manner to influence your verdict. Your
ultimate verdict would be reached solely

and entirely upon the evidence that you
hear from the witness stand and the law
that the Court will give you at the conclusion of all the case, and we will
admonish you from time to time in the
event anyone should endeavor to talk to
you about the case, that means any person,
whether it be court officials, elevator
operator, or anyone, you are instructed
to immediately advise the Court.

You should not in any manner allow
either sympathy or prejudice to in any
manner influence your verdict. Your ultimate verdict will be reached solely and
from the evidence that you hear from the
witness stand and the law that the Court
will give you at the conclusion of all of
the evidence.

You may proceed with the voir dire
examination.

> (Thereupon the jury was examined
> upon their voir dire by counsel
> for the State and the Defense,
> and continued until twelve
> jurors had been accepted by
> counsel for the State and the
> Defense, whereupon said jury
> was sworn to try the issues in
> this cause.)

THE COURT: Ladies and gentlemen, we
will recess until one o'clock tomorrow.
Report back into the jury room in the rear
of this courtroom. Good evening.

> (Thereupon said cause was con-
> tinued until the following day,
> Tuesday, December 15, 1970, at
> 1:00 o'clock P.M.)

THE PEOPLE OF THE)
STATE OF ILLINOIS)
)
    vs.   )
)
DONALD PAYNE   )

                        Before Judge Richard
                        J. Fitzgerald and a
                        jury
                        Tuesday, December 15,
                        1970
                        1:00 o'clock P.M.

    Court convened pursuant to adjourn-
ment.

    PRESENT:
        MR. WALTER J. PARRISH and
        MR. JOSEPH PODUSKA,
            Assistant State's Attorneys,
            appeared for the People;
        MR. CONSTANTINE P. XINOS,
            Assistant Public Defender,
            appeared for the Defendant.

THE CLERK: People versus Donald Payne.

MR. XINOS: Judge, before we bring the jury out, just for the record I make certain anticipatory objections. I am not sure of the propriety of them but I would rather make them. I object to the exhibition of any physical evidence prior to the time the State attempts to introduce it. I believe I have a valid objection to the introduction of it and I think whatever objections I have is that if they are sustained would be to no avail if the jury is permitted to see a weapon sitting at the table.

THE COURT: I am sure the State would keep it under cover anyway.

MR. PARRISH: If that is the purport of the objection—

THE COURT: Yes.

MR. XINOS: I would further request that the Court, upon hearing evidence, if it deems the evidence is such that it would be proper in the motion to suppress that was filed before the trial, that it would consider the motion to suppress reopened and if necessary rule again on the motion to suppress, if anything revealing comes up during the testimony with either the officers or the complaining witness.

MR. PARRISH: We would object to that. I mean that is the burden of the defendant, if he believes now that he would make a proper and timely objection—

THE COURT: Well, I would say that—

MR. XINOS: I am not going to object to it.

THE COURT: But in the event that evidence should be forthcoming during the course of the trial which would by necessity compel the Court to entertain a motion at any time during the course of the trial that the evidence was illegally obtained, it was obtained in violation of the constitutional rights of the defendant, then at that time I would certainly entertain a motion of the defendant to suppress any evidence which was seized illegally or any motions that you would want to bring about.

MR. PARRISH: That is the basis of the State's objection, that the defendant would have to be a moving party, and we certainly would not hope that he places the burden upon the Court to make a determination—

THE COURT: That would be improper but we would entertain the motion at the time that the evidence would indicate that constitutional rights were violated.

MR. XINOS: Thank you. I have one final thing and that is that the Court is aware from the motions to suppress the evidence which led to the arrest of the defendant is based largely on hearsay, which of course is not objectionable in probable cause hearing, but in the determination of

guilt or innocence would be objectionable, and it may be prejudicial by the
very questions despite the fact that objection to the questions may be sustained.

I just anticipate those kind of questions as part of the State's duty in the
prosecution of the case and I object to
them beforehand and ask the Court just to
make note of my objection in case—

THE COURT: Very well.

MR. PARRISH: That is a misstatement of
fact that evidence in the motion to suppress showed clearly an accomplice who was
a juvenile implicated the defendant.

THE COURT: Well, when we reach that
stage as to what another party said—

MR. PARRISH: He is available. That is
what we indicate to the Court.

THE COURT: If he is going to testify
then of course there is no question at
all. Bring out the jury.

MR. XINOS: I ask that the witnesses be
excluded.

THE COURT: All witnesses in the matter
of the People of the State of Illinois
versus Donald Payne will be excluded from
the courtroom until called upon to
testify.

MR. PARRISH: We join in that motion,
Judge.

        (Thereupon the following pro-
        ceedings were had within the
        presence and hearing of the
        jury.)

THE COURT: You may proceed, Counsel.

OPENING STATEMENT
BY MR. PARRISH:

May it please the Court, the defendant,
Mr. Xinos, my partner, Mr. Poduska, and
ladies and gentlemen of the jury. At this
time the People of the State of Illinois
have an opportunity because we do have
that burden of proof in the case to appear
before you and indicate to you what we
believe the evidence will show by compe-
tent and credible testimony from the witness stand.

The evidence will show, ladies and
gentlemen, on August 4, 1970, somewhere
shortly after 9 P.M. on that day in question, one of the State's witnesses, Mr.
Castelli, was one of the owners of a
liquor store located on the near west side
of Chicago; that he was employed on that
date in question along with a fellow employee, Mr. DeAngelo, and were doing business at about that time of day or night.

The evidence will further show from the
witness stand that no other patrons were
in the liquor establishment at that time
of the day or night and Mr. Castelli was
removing certain moneys from the cash
register.

The evidence will further show that he
removed approximately two or three hundred
dollars from the cash register and was
placing it in his pocket for delivery to
some safekeeping. That at about that time
of the day or night two persons entered
the liquor establishment.

The evidence will further show that Mr.

Castelli and his fellow employee were
standing in approximately the middle area
of the counter of the liquor store. That
at that time a person now known as the
defendant Donald Payne appeared approximately two or three feet in front of him
across the counter.

The evidence will further show there
were two cash registers in that liquor
store, one at the end of the counter and
one approximately at the end of the
counter at which Mr. Castelli was
standing.

The evidence will further show that the
defendant Donald Payne, with a weapon in
his hand, stated to Mr. Castelli, and in
the presence of Mr. DeAngelo, that "I want
that money," indicating that the money
that Mr. Castelli had just removed from
the cash register and was attempting
to place in his pocket.

The evidence will further show that Mr.
Castelli tried to back away from that area
where he saw the gun and at that time
another party came around and apprehended
him.

The evidence will further show by the
testimony of Mr. DeAngelo from the witness
stand that at the time Mr. Castelli attempted to back away the defendant Donald
Payne used certain curse words and extended an arm forward with the pistol in
his hand and attempted to fire the pistol,
pulling the trigger three or four times,
and each occasion both persons, Mr.
Castelli and Mr. DeAngelo, could hear the

pull of that trigger and click of the
gun.

The evidence will further show, frustrated in their actions to rob the liquor
store and frustrated with the fact that
Mr. Castelli had attempted to conceal the
money, the defendant Donald Payne and
his accomplice fled from the scene.

The evidence will further show by com-
petent and credible testimony from the
witness stand that shortly on that day in
question the defendant Donald Payne was
arrested.

We believe that evidence along with
other evidence that you will hear from the
witness stand will be sufficient for you
to find the defendant Donald Payne guilty
of attempt armed robbery and attempt
murder beyond a reasonable doubt. Thank
you.

OPENING STATEMENT
BY MR. XINOS:

Your Honor, ladies and gentlemen, what
Mr. Parrish has indicated to you is not
evidence. It may be what he expects to
prove, it may be what he hopes to prove,
but it is certainly not proof.

The only proof in this case is going to
come from the witnesses who testify from
that stand under oath.

We talked yesterday just briefly about
the presumption of innocence and none of
you had any quarrel with that presumption.
You all agreed in our conversation that
throughout this trial you would continue

to presume the defendant to be innocent
unless and until the State convinced you
beyond all reasonable doubt that he was
not.

This presumption of innocence is probably the greatest single protection that
any legal system has ever afforded any
individual. Because of that this defendant Donald Payne and every other
person accused of crime is not required
to present evidence in the case.

He is not required to testify. He is
not required to ask questions. He can sit
during his trial and not participate at
all and rightfully expect the State to
carry its burden if they can to proving
him guilty.

The defendant is going to testify. A
witness will testify in his behalf
and, without going into the specifics of
the testimony because you will hear it
from the stand, the evidence will show
that on the night of this robbery that is
supposed to have occurred between six-
thirty in the evening and eight or nine
o'clock the following morning when he was
arrested in his home that the defendant
was either at his home or within ten doors
from his home during that entire time.

You will also learn from the testimony
of not only Donald Payne and his witness
but also the testimony of police officers
that the distance between Donald Payne's
home where he lived with his family and
the place at which this robbery occurred
is between four and five miles.

You will further hear testimony from the

State witnesses that when they arrested
Donald Payne he was at home in bed. At
that time the police came in, they
searched him, they searched his bed, they
searched his room, and found absolutely
nothing to connect him with this crime.

Equally important is the State's evidence which will include testimony of Mr.
Castelli who is an owner of a liquor
store. Right after this robbery Mr.
Castelli talked to the police and you will
hear either from his testimony or from
the testimony of the officers what Mr.
Castelli said concerning the people who
had perpetrated this armed robbery and
that will include hopefully the description of the two robbers which he gave
the police at that time.

You will see from that description that
it is a most general description, not
specific. It is the kind of description
that could fit a hundred to a thousand
or ten thousand male young Negroes in this
city, but you will see that even with
that general description, through your
own observations, through the testimony
of the defendant, and if necessary through
the records of the County Jail, that the
general description given by Mr. Castelli
after this crime in no way fits this defendant.

All I ask is that you wait until you
hear the State's case and our case and
then the Judge will instruct you before
beginning to decide whether the State has
carried its burden. Thank you.

THE COURT: Proceed.

MR. PARRISH: We will call Mr. DeAngelo, please.

FRED DEANGELO,
a witness called on behalf of the People, having been first duly sworn, was examined and testified as follows:

DIRECT EXAMINATION
BY MR. PARRISH:

Q Now would you state your full and complete name, sir?

A Fred DeAngelo.

Q And would you spell your first and last name for the Court and jury?

A Fred, F-r-e-d, DeAngelo, D-e-A-n-g-e-l-o.

Q Would you sit back in your seat, sir, and hold the microphone up to your mouth and speak out so the Court and jury can hear you. Where are you employed, Mr. DeAngelo?

A A liquor store.

Q And do you now know the name of that liquor store?

A Shop-Rite Liquors.

Q You have to speak up louder, sir.

A Shop-Rite Liquors.

Q How long, if at all, have you been so employed at that liquor establishment?

A About four years.

Q And were you so employed at that establishment on August 4, 1970?

A I was.

Q And in what capacity were you employed?

A A liquor clerk.

Q   What time of day or night did your
tour or duty on August 4, 1970, start?

A   From three in the afternoon until
closing, approximately eleven-thirty.

Q   And were you so employed at that company at or about 9 P.M. on August 4, 1970?

A   I was.

Q   And who, if anyone, was present in
that establishment with you at that time
of day or night?

A   Mr. Castelli.

Q   Do you know his first name?

A   Joseph.

Q   And in what capacity—strike that.
What relationship, if any, does he have to
that liquor establishment?

A   He is the president of the organization.

Q   Now shortly after 9 P.M. on that day
in question did anything unusual occur
in that liquor establishment?

A   We were attempted to be robbed, sir.

Q   Did anything unusual occur?   The
answer is yes or no.

A   Yes.

Q   And what, if anything, unusual happened shortly after 9 P.M. on August 4,
1970?

A   There was an attempted robbery in the
store.

Q   Were there any other persons in that
store other than yourself and Joseph
Castelli close to 9 P.M. on August 4,
1970?

A   Did you mean other employees?

Q   Anybody.   At or around 9 P.M. was

there anyone other than yourself in that
store?

A We had two men come in, yes, sir.

Q And were there any other persons
other than you and Joseph Castelli and
these other two persons who came in?

A No, sir.

Q And would you describe the two persons who came into the store at or about
that time?

A Two young colored fellows. One was
rather short and the defendant.

Q When you say the defendant are you
referring to—

A Mr. Payne.

Q And do you see any of the persons who
came into that liquor establishment on
August 4, 1970, in court today?

A Yes, sir, Mr. Payne.

Q Would you point him out, please?

A There.

MR. PARRISH: Would the record indicate,
your Honor, that the witness is identifying the defendant, Donald Payne.

THE COURT: Yes.

MR. PARRISH: Q What, if anything, did
you see the defendant Donald Payne do
after he came into that liquor establishment?

A As he entered the door he had a
pistol in his hand.

Q And would you describe for the Court
and jury where you were at the time he
entered the door?

A I was at the right-hand side of the
register which faces on the counter.

Q And in what direction were you facing, north, east, south, or west?

A I was facing east.

Q And in what direction did Mr. Payne enter the door, if you can recall?

A From the south.

Q How far, if at all, was Donald Payne from you when you first saw him with the gun in his possession?

A As he entered the store door, sir.

Q And approximately how many feet, if you can recall?

A Oh, I would say approximately eight to ten feet.

Q And did Mr. Payne ever get any closer to you than eight or ten feet?

A Yes, sir, he stood across the counter from me which is approximately two foot.

Q And who, if anyone, was near you at that time?

A Mr. Castelli.

Q And on what side of you was Mr. Castelli at the time that Donald Payne stood immediately in front of you?

A On my left, sir.

Q What, if anything, was Mr. Castelli doing, if you can recall, when Donald Payne entered the store?

A Mr. Castelli had just taken the total amount of money out of the register and was sorting it and going to put it into his pocket when Mr. Payne walked in the store.

Q To the best of your knowledge do you know approximately how much money was taken out of the register by Mr. Castelli?

A I would say several hundred dollars.

Q Now as Mr. Payne stood facing you
while you were near Mr. Castelli who was
removing money from the cash register, did
Mr. Payne say anything?

A "I want that."

Q And who was he looking at, if at all,
at the time that he made that statement?

A Mr. Castelli.

Q What, if anything, did Mr. Castelli
do after hearing that statement?

A Mr. Castelli put the money into his
pocket and that is when Mr. Payne said,
"I want that," as he was putting it into
his pocket, I should say.

Q What happened next in respect to—

A Mr. Castelli—

Q Excuse me.

A Mr. Castelli backed out around the
small el in the counter.

Q And what, if anything, did Donald
Payne do after Mr. Castelli started back-
ing away?

A Mr. Payne muttered a word and reached
over and attempted to shoot Mr. Castelli.

Q When you say that he reached over
and attempted to shoot Mr. Castelli would
you describe for the Court exactly what
Donald Payne did at that time?

A He pulled a gun—the trigger on the
gun three times.

Q And where was his hand or arm at the
time that he did that?

A An arm extended.

Q Would you demonstrate that for the
Court and jury, sir?

A Such.

Q Let the record reflect the witness

extended his right arm as though leaning
over the counter. What happened, if at
all—did Mr. Payne have the gun, if you
can recall?

A His right hand.

Q And about how many times if you can
recall was the trigger pulled?

A Three times.

Q You mentioned that he uttered a word.
Do you recall at this time what that
word was?

A Yes, sir.

Q Would you tell the Court and jury
exactly what Donald Payne said to the best
of your recollection?

A Motherfucker.

Q And who was he looking at when he
said that?

A Mr. Castelli.

Q What happened next, to the best of
your recollection?

A Mr. Castelli—when the gun failed to
go off Mr. Payne and this other gentleman
broke and ran. Mr. Castelli tried to
catch the second young man and hit the
counter and was knocked down.

Q What happened next, if you can
recall?

A They ran out the store. Mr. Castelli
and I ran out after them.

Q Now would you tell the Court and jury
what the lighting conditions were in that
liquor establishment on that day in
question?

A There are four banks of lights, two
on each side of the store, it's a double
store, two on each of the store with four

elements in each light and they run from
one end of the store to the opposite end.

Q Now when Mr. Payne came into that
establishment did you have an occasion to
observe him from the first time he came
in until the time he left?

A I did.

Q Approximately how long did he remain
in that liquor establishment, if you know?

A I would say about four, five minutes,
sir.

Q During the course of that time did
any other patrons or customers come into
the liquor establishment?

A No, sir.

Q How many people during the course of
that four or five minutes was in the
store other than yourself and Mr.
Castelli?

A None except the defendants.

Q And what would that total number of
persons be?

A Four people.

Q Can you describe for the Court and
jury the weapon that you saw in the hand
of Donald Payne on that day in question?

A A small-caliber pistol.

Q Could you describe the color?

A It was sort of dark steel.

Q And approximately how long, if you
can recall, from the butt to the tip of
the weapon would that be?

A Oh, about not quite the size of your
hand, sir.

Q Indicating from the palm to the tip
of the finger?

A Right.

MR. PARRISH: We ask at this time, Your Honor, that this exhibit be marked as People's Exhibit No. 1 for identification.

   (Thereupon said object was so
    marked as People's Exhibit
    No. 1 for identification.)

MR. PARRISH: Q Mr. DeAngelo, I show you what has been marked as People's Exhibit No. 1 for identification and ask you to observe this exhibit. Have you looked at it?

A Yes, sir.

Q You have to speak louder now.

A Yes, sir.

Q And Mr. DeAngelo, I ask you whether or not People's Exhibit No. 1 appears substantially similar to the weapon that you saw on August 4, 1970?

A It does, sir.

Q Does it appear to look like the weapon that you saw on August 4, 1970, in respect to color?

A Yes, sir.

Q Does it appear to look like the weapon that you saw on August 4, 1970, somewhere after 9 P.M., insofar as size is concerned?

A Physically the same.

Q And does this weapon truly and correctly represent in appearance the weapon similar to the one that you saw on August 4, 1970?

A Yes, it does, sir.

Q That tavern is located at 1644 West 79 Street in the city of Chicago, is that correct?

A Yes, sir.

Q And it is in Cook County?

A Yes, sir.

Q And all you have testified to happened in Cook County, in the city of Chicago, is that correct?

A Yes, sir.

MR. PARRISH: You may inquire.

CROSS-EXAMINATION
BY MR. XINOS:

Q Sir, you testified that you have been employed by Mr. Castelli for about four years, is that correct?

A Yes, sir.

Q Is that your full-time job?

A Yes, sir.

Q Prior to that time where did you work?

A I worked for a heating company.

Q How many other employees did Mr. Castelli have, if you know?

MR. PARRISH: Objection, insofar as the vagueness. If he is talking about the period of time—

MR. XINOS: Q During August of 1970.

A I would say approximately seven or eight, all told, sir.

Q Was this night that you were working, the night in which this attempted armed robbery occurred, is this your regular work night?

A Yes, sir, it was.

Q Sir, prior to August of 1970 have you ever seen Donald Payne before?

A No, I have not, sir.

Q Did you see him the day after this

attempted armed robbery in the police station, didn't you?

A I did.

Q At that time were you with Mr. Castelli or were you by yourself?

A I was with Mr. Castelli.

Q You went together to the police station?

A Right.

Q And what time approximately was that that you and Mr. Castelli got there?

A I would say approximately—well, I don't know exactly when we got there. I would say approximately one o'clock.

Q How far is it from the front door of the store to the point where you were standing when the two men came in?

A About eight to ten foot, sir.

Q Eight to ten feet?

A Right.

Q When people came into the store what was the first thing that they did? By that I mean where did these people go?

A They came right up to the register, sir.

Q They walked up to the register or did they run up to the register?

A They kind of came in rather quickly. That is all. Not running, not a slow walk either, a fast pace.

Q A fast pace?

A Yes.

Q How many seconds would you say it took from the time that the door was open and the two men came in up until the time they stopped in front of the counter, approximately?

A   Oh, five, eight, ten seconds, something like that. I wouldn't venture to say. I was looking at the pistol.

Q   Were you looking at the pistol during the substantial time of this attempted armed robbery?

A   Well, he had it pointed directly at me originally.

Q   Did you at any time see more than one hand on this pistol?

A   No, sir.

Q   Are you familiar with weapons?

A   I don't handle them if that is what you mean.

Q   You testified that you saw the robber squeeze the trigger, is that correct?

A   Right.

Q   At the time that the trigger was being squeezed how many hands were on the gun?

A   One.

Q   Did you hear or see the trigger being pulled?

A   I heard the click.

Q   Did you hear anything at the time that the man pulled the trigger again?

A   There was three definite clicks.

Q   In between the first time that the man pulled the trigger and the last time that the man pulled the trigger did he still have just the one hand on the gun?

A   One hand on the pistol.

Q   Did you look at the shorter man who came into the store?

A   Did I look at him?

Q   Yes.

A   I saw them both.

Q Did you get as good a look at the smaller man as you did the larger man?

A No, sir.

Q Sir?

A No, sir.

Q Why was that, sir?

A Because the man had the gun on me and the other one walked around the other end of the store, around the counter.

Q When the men walked in was Mr. Castelli in front of the register that he was taking the money out of?

A He was to the left of the register, I was to the right, exactly.

Q When the man walked up to the register which was near you how much time passed before anything was said to Mr. Castelli?

A As the man came into the door and up to the counter Mr. Castelli had just put the money into his pocket and this man said, "I want that."

Q At that time did Mr. Castelli move in any direction?

A Yes, sir.

Q Did he move away from you or toward you?

A He moved away from me.

Q And what is located away from you? Is there an office or a safe?

A No, sir, it's a small el in the counter.

Q And at that time what did the taller man do, that is the man with the gun? Did he follow Mr. Castelli?

A No, sir, he stayed with me.

Q What happened next?

A   As Mr. Castelli got around toward the end of the counter the other man said, "Get him."

Q   From the time that the taller man first spoke to Mr. Castelli up until the time Mr. Castelli got around the counter how many seconds would you say had passed?

A   It's rather difficult to say.

Q   Well, would you say three, four, five seconds?

A   I would say a little more than that.

Q   Was Mr. Castelli walking or running?

A   He was walking. In fact, he was kind of back out.

Q   Did he start to walk as soon as the taller man indicated that he wanted the money?

A   Did he start to walk the minute—

Q   Well—

A   He started to back out from around the end of the counter.

Q   And when he started to back out is that when the shorter man said something?

A   Yes, the shorter man got around the end of the counter, he got close to Mr. Castelli, and Mr. Castelli turned around and he said to this fellow here, "Get him."

Q   And at that time you heard three clicks?

A   Then Mr. Payne reached over and pulled the gun three times.

Q   And then the two men left?

A   Yes, sir.

Q   Sir, did you talk with the police officers—withdraw that. Did you call the police after this?

A   The police were called, right, sir.

Q   And how long after the two men had left the store did the police arrive?

A   I would say approximately ten minutes, maybe.

Q   And at that time did you have a conversation with them?

A   With the police officer?

Q   Yes.

A   I didn't personally. They were talking to Mr. Castelli.

Q   Did you ever have a conversation with the police officers on that evening about what had occurred?

A   Well, mentioned the robbery, I mean the attempted robbery and so forth, yes.

Q   When you gave this account of what happened to the police was Mr. Castelli there also?

A   Yes.

Q   And was he situated at a place or a point where he could hear what you were saying and you could hear what he was saying?

A   Within the vicinity of the store, yes, sir.

Q   Did you at that time give a description of either or both men to members of the Chicago Police Department?

A   Yes, sir.

Q   Do you recall at that time how tall you said the men were?

A   Approximately one was approximately my height and the other was shorter.

Q   And how tall are you, sir?

A   About six foot.

Q   How much do you weigh?

A About 148 right now. I just got out of the hospital.

Q Do you recall giving any other description of either of the two men that had come into the store to rob you?

A What do you mean?

Q Well, do you recall giving the police the weight or the build of the men that had come in, starting with the shorter man?

A I would say all I would say one was shorter than the other, one was taller and one was shorter, sir.

Q Did you give the police any idea as to the kind of build or physique that either of the two men had?

A As I said, the one man was about my physical size.

Q In height?

A Height and weight.

Q And how much did you weigh at that time?

A About 155.

Q Do you remember now whether you told the police that the taller man had come in your store was about—

MR. PARRISH: Objection.

THE COURT: Sustained.

MR. XINOS: What is the nature of the objection?

MR. PARRISH: Judge—

THE COURT: Rephrase your question.

MR. XINOS: Q Sir, did you indicate to the police on the night of the attempt robbery how much taller of the two robbers weighed in your opinion?

A How much—

MR. PARRISH: Objection again, Judge. We ask for a side bar conference.

> (Thereupon a side bar conference was had outside the hearing of the jury after which the following proceedings were had within the presence and hearing of the jury.)

MR. XINOS: Q Sir, you testified that you told the police that the taller of the two men that came into the liquor store was about your height?

A Right.

Q And you further testified that you are approximately six feet tall, is that correct?

A Right.

Q Do you recall whether you told any police officer on that evening how much you thought the taller of the two men weighed?

A Not necessarily, sir. I just said more or less my physical size.

Q Do you know at that time whether the police officers with whom you were speaking were taking notes or writing any of this down?

A No, I don't, sir.

Q Do you recall the names of the officers that came to the liquor store?

A Officer Higgins.

Q Was there another officer with him?

A Mr. Cullen, I believe. I don't know exactly.

Q Were they both present at the time that you were giving this information, sir?

A I was busy at the counter taking care
of customers at this time. I was in a
routine of trying to take care of people
that were still in the store while Mr.
Castelli and the officers were talking and
I would chime in occasionally when I had
the opportunity.

Q Did you provide any further description of either of the two men that came
into the store other than the description
that you have given us here?

A No, sir.

Q To the best of your knowledge, sir,
you don't know at this time whether that
gun that you saw was loaded or unloaded,
is that correct?

A No, I couldn't tell you.

Q And this clip that Mr. Parrish showed
you marked as People's Exhibit One for
identification, you didn't see this clip
at that time, did you?

A No, I did not.

MR. XINOS: Nothing further. Thank you,
sir.

MR. PARRISH: No redirect. Thank you.
                    (Witness excused.)

MR. PARRISH: Call Mr. Castelli.

JOSEPH CASTELLI

a witness called on behalf of the People,
having been first duly sworn, was examined
and testified as follows:

DIRECT EXAMINATION
BY MR. PARRISH:

Q Now would you state your full and
complete name, sir?

A Joseph Castelli.

Q You have to hold the microphone up so that you can be heard out in the court-room. Would you repeat your name?

A Joseph Castelli.

Q Would you spell both your first and last name?

A J-o-s-e-p-h C-a-s-t-e-l-l-i.

Q Now Mr. Castelli, what is your business or occupation?

A I own a liquor store.

Q What is the name of that liquor store?

A Shop-Rite Liquors.

Q And for how long have you been em-ployed at that particular location in the city of Chicago?

A Twenty-four years.

Q Twenty-four years?

A Yes, sir.

Q And is that liquor store now incor-porated or sole proprietorship?

A This is a corporation, sir.

Q And who are the shareholders in that corporation?

MR. XINOS: Objection to relevancy of it, Judge. There is no requirement of ownership as an element of the crime.

THE COURT: Sustained.

MR. PARRISH: Q Well, on August 4, 1970, was that business incorporated?

A Yes, sir.

Q And were you an officer of that cor-poration?

A Yes, sir.

Q And what capacity?

A President.

Q Were you in that location on August 4, 1970, sir?

A Yes, sir.

Q You have to speak louder, sir.

A Yes, sir.

Q What time of day or night did you arrive at that location on August 4, 1970?

A I didn't get you.

Q What time of day or night did you arrive in your liquor store on August 4, 1970?

A I usually arrive there around three-thirty, a quarter to four.

Q Is that P.M. or A.M.?

A P.M.

Q And were you in that store at or about 9 P.M. on August 4, 1970?

A Yes, I was, sir.

Q And who was in that store with you, if anyone?

A Mr. Fred DeAngelo.

Q And what capacity was Mr. Fred DeAngelo in that particular store on that day in question?

A He is employed as a clerk, sir.

Q And were there any other employees in that store at or about that time other than you and Mr. DeAngelo?

A No, sir.

Q Now shortly after 9 P.M. on August 4, 1970, did anything unusual happen in your business? Did anything happen that was out of the ordinary after 9 P.M.?

A About ten after nine the gentleman walked in.

Q And the gentleman you are speaking of, is that the defendant Donald Payne?

A   Yes, sir.

Q   And was he alone or with someone when he walked into your business establishment?

A   He was with another young man.

Q   Could you describe as best you can recall how the other person appeared in relationship to Donald Payne?

A   Well, he was much shorter and his clothing was sort of on the beige color, he was a much shorter and younger man.

Q   Now when Donald Payne and his companion walked into your business somewhere near 9 P.M. on August 4, 1970, did you observe anything in Donald Payne's hand or about his person?

A   Yes, I did.

Q   What, if anything, did you observe?

A   He had a small-caliber pistol.

Q   And would you describe the small caliber pistol that you indicate Donald Payne had on August 4, 1970?

A   Well, I would say maybe a .25 automatic or something like that. I couldn't really be sure but it was a pistol.

Q   Could you describe as best you can recall the color of that pistol that you observed on August 4, 1970?

A   That blue steel.

Q   And could you approximate the length or size of that pistol as you saw it on that day in question?

A   All I could say it was a small caliber, sir.

Q   When you first observed Donald Payne where was he in relationship to the door of your business?

A I was in front of the register and
Mr. DeAngelo was maybe a foot or so away
from me on my right and Mr. Payne was
in front of Mr. DeAngelo when I first
noticed him.

Q In relationship to the door of your
business, how far away was Donald Payne
at the time when you first observed him?

A A good six, seven feet away from the
door.

Q The person who walked in with Donald
Payne, was he even with Donald Payne at
that time or was one in front or back
of the other, if you can recall?

A The other fellow came in first and
Donald Payne was in back of him, as I recall now, because I hadn't seen them
come in.

Q What, if anything, were you doing at
the time that Donald Payne and his accomplice came into that store?

A I was taking money out of the register, sir.

Q How many registers, by the way, are
located in your store?

A There are two, one close to the door
and one further away from the door, and
I was at the one further away from the
door.

Q For the benefit of the Court and jury
would you describe the layout of your
store inside?

A It's a counter and it's an el-shaped
counter.

Q Speak louder so the Court and the
jury can hear you.

A It's an el-shaped counter. There is

one register maybe three, four feet away
from the front door and the other one
maybe about ten or twelve feet away, and
we were in between the two registers.
Then there is a little el. The register
is here and the el comes this way and
that is the counter also.

Q When a person comes into your store
in which direction does he proceed as
he enters your door?

A Well, he comes—he comes—

Q South, north, east, or west?

A Well, there is two doors, the entrance—there is a counter in between and
he comes in the other entrance, but Mr.
Payne didn't come in the other entrance,
he came in the door where people check out
and go out the door.

Q The doors to your business, do they
face if you are going out the door, do
they face east, north, south, or west?

A Well, the store faces north and south
and the door going out opens going south.

Q So a person comes into the store he
is going north?

A Right, sir.

Q And the counters in your store, do
they run north and south?

A Yes, sir.

Q And the cash registers then, the back
portion of the cash register faces in
what direction?

A Like it faces east, I would face the
register east.

Q So when you first saw Mr. Payne in
what direction were you facing?

A I was facing east.

Q And in what direction was Mr. Payne facing when you first saw him with the gun in his hand?

A Facing me and that would be facing west.

Q Now how close, if at all, did Donald Payne ever come to you physically in feet?

A The closest I would say is three, four feet.

Q And during that time did you ever hear Donald Payne speak?

A All I heard him say, "Give me that."

Q What, if anything, were you doing at the time that Donald Payne said, "Give me that"?

A I was putting money in my pocket.

Q And was Mr. Payne looking at you when he made that statement and were you looking at him?

A Well, when he said that I looked at him.

Q What, if anything, did you do after Donald Payne made that statement?

A I edged away from the register.

Q When you say you edged away did you go forward toward Donald Payne?

A I backed up, sir.

Q And what, if anything, next occurred in respect to you and Donald Payne?

A As I was edging back the other lad came up to me and he said, "Shoot him, shoot him, shoot him."

Q The other person came up to you and said, "Shoot him"?

A Yes, he came around the counter, he came close to me.

Q And do you know who the other person

was talking to when he made that statement?

A He was talking to Mr. Payne.

Q What, if anything, did Donald Payne
do after the accomplice said, "Shoot him,
shoot him"?

A He raised his arm and pointed the gun
at me and fired three times or four—at
least I heard three clicks.

Q And what, if anything, were you doing
at the time Donald Payne was pulling the
trigger three or four times?

A I just stood there, I stopped.

Q Were you observing Donald Payne at
that time?

A As much as I could.

Q And from the time that you first saw
Donald Payne until the time you left your
store were you able to observe him?

A As much as I could, sir, enough to
identify him.

MR. XINOS: Object to that.

THE COURT: Sustained.

MR. PARRISH: Q Were there any other
persons in your store at the time that
Donald Payne and his accomplice was there
along with you and your employee?

A No, just Mr. DeAngelo.

Q Approximately how long did all of
this activity take when Donald Payne was
in your store?

A Two, three, four minutes.

Q And would you describe the lighting
conditions of your store, to the best of
your recollection?

A The store is very well lit because we

have to display merchandise and it has
to be well lit.

Q Approximately how much money did you
have in your possession transferring to
your pocket at the time Donald Payne said,
"I want that"?

A I couldn't really give you an exact
figure but I would say around two hundred
and fifty to three hundred dollars.

Q Would you tell the Court and jury how
the front of your store is made in respect
to visibility?

A We have four large windows approximately eight foot in length so anybody
can see in. They're very large windows
and two doors coming in—one coming in and
one going out.

Q These are commonly referred to as
plate glass windows?

A Plate glass, yes.

Q You can see out of those windows, is
that correct?

A Yes, sir.

Q Now do you see the person now in the
courtroom who you allege that you saw on
August 4, 1970, with the gun in his hand
shortly after nine?

A Yes, I do, sir.

Q And would you point him out, please?

A That is Donald Payne.

Q And would the record reflect that the
witness is identifying the defendant,
Donald Payne. I will show you what has
been marked heretofore as People's Exhibit
No. 1 for identification and I ask you to
observe this exhibit. Have you observed
that exhibit?

A   This is the gun similar to that, sir.

Q   And when and where and under what circumstances did you first see a gun similar to People's Exhibit No. 1?

A   When he said, "Give me that," I looked up and that is what I saw.

Q   What day and what year was that, if you can recall?

A   That was August the 4, sir.

Q   Now does that gun appear to look like the gun that you saw on August 4, 1970, shortly after 9 P.M., similar in color, shape, and size?

A   Yes, sir.

MR. PARRISH: Thank you. You may inquire.

CROSS-EXAMINATION
BY MR. XINOS:

Q   Mr. Castelli, where were the two robbers when you first became aware that someone other than yourself and your employee were in the store? Where were they standing?

A   They were standing right in front of Mr. DeAngelo and I was in front of the register.

Q   And at that point did—

A   I didn't see them come in, I just saw him standing there when he announced himself.

Q   When the announcement was made where did you go or what did you do?

A   I just backed—I was putting money in my pocket and I just backed away.

Q And could you approximate in distance how many feet or inches you backed away?

A Like I say I really don't know how far. I would say three or four feet I backed up. I don't know exactly.

Q Did you back up immediately when you heard this command?

A Yes, I did. I just stepped back.

Q When you inched back did you stop?

A Then I stopped.

Q What happened when you stopped?

A The other lad had run up to me and he said, "Shoot him, shoot him."

Q Would you tell us now if you can remember approximately how long in seconds it took you to back up to the point where you were in front of the register or behind the register to the point where you stopped and the short man came up and said, "Shoot him"?

A I would say a minute or so. I really don't know. I couldn't give you an account of how many minutes. A minute or two. I really don't know.

Q When you first saw the man did you immediately begin to back away?

A When he announced himself then I did.

Q The total distance you backed away was less than five feet, would you say?

A I would say five, four, I couldn't really, I didn't measure it.

Q And as soon as you stopped is that when the shorter man said, "Shoot him," or whatever he said?

A Yes.

Q And at that point is that when you heard the sound?

A Yes, sir.

Q How many sounds did you hear coming from this weapon?

A Three, at least three, maybe four.

Q What did the sound sound like?

A A click, a loud click.

Q At that time were you looking at the gun or were you looking at the smaller man, the larger man, or somewhere else?

A I was looking at him.

Q At that time did you see one or more hands on that gun?

A Only one, sir. I didn't see any—he held the gun and just stuck it out like that.

Q After the shorter man said, "Shoot him," did the larger man immediately begin pulling the trigger?

A Yes, sir.

Q And was that trigger pulled in rapid succession—click—click—click?

A Yes, sir.

Q Would you say the pulling of the trigger took two or three seconds?

A Steady.

Q No, I mean the three clicks.

A One right after another.

Q After the third click what, if anything, did the shorter man and the taller man do?

A After the clicks they both ran out. He ran out first and the other little man right after him.

Q How far was it from the point where you were when you heard the clicks to your front door at that time?

A Where I was?

Q Yes, sir. Would you say fifteen feet?

A At least fifteen feet.

Q Sir, did you call the police after this happened?

A No, I didn't. Somebody else did and I don't know who.

Q Did the police come to your business?

A Five, ten minutes later.

Q And did you have a conversation with those policemen?

A Yes, I did.

Q Do you know now whether that was Officer Cullen or Officer Higgins?

A Yes, sir.

Q You recognize those officers to see them again?

A Yes, sir.

Q Were you asked at that time by either or both of those officers to give an account of what happened?

A Yes.

MR. PARRISH: Objection. The State has a continuing objection.

THE COURT: It will be so noted.

MR. XINOS: Q Sir, were you asked?

A Yes, I was.

Q Were you asked also to give a description as best you could of the two men that had come into your store?

A Yes.

Q And did you give a description?

A Yes.

Q Do you recall now what you told the officers regarding the height and weight of the shorter man?

A I can't really say what I said right

now. I gave them a fair description as
to their clothing, to the height, five-
five, five-six, or something like that.

Q　In regard to the taller man did you
give a description of the taller man to
the police?

A　Yes, I did.

Q　Do you remember how tall you said he
was?

A　Close to six, five-eleven, five-ten,
I really don't know what I told them.

Q　Do you recall giving the police a
weight which you thought the taller man
weighed, how much, did you tell—

A　I don't think they asked me that. I
really don't know.

Q　Isn't it a fact that you told Officer
Higgins and Officer Cullen at that time
that the taller of the two men was 185
pounds, is your opinion—

MR. PARRISH:　Objection to this. This
is improper.

THE COURT:　If he can, he may answer.

THE WITNESS:　I can't recall right now.

MR. XINOS:　Q　Do you recall if you did
give any—

A　Maybe I did, sir, but I can't—

Q　Do you recall if you described any
features of either of the two men?

A　As far as their clothing and as far
as features—

Q　You have to say yes or no. Do you
recall giving the police a description of
the features of either of the two men?

A　One was short and one was tall. What
else can I say?

Q　Do you recall telling the police

whether there were any facial characteristics that you noticed of either of the two men?

A Pertaining to what, sir? If he was white or colored or what?

Q You had indicated to them that both of the men were Negroes, is that correct?

A Right, sir.

Q And you had indicated to them the approximate age, is that correct?

A Approximately, yes.

Q You testified when Mr. Parrish was asking the questions that the shorter man appeared to be younger, is that correct?

A Yes.

Q At the time you spoke to the police officers do you recall telling the police officers that the shorter man was between twenty and twenty-two and the taller man was between nineteen and twenty-one?

A I might have.

Q Do you recall telling the police officers at that time anything else about the description of either men?

A Only their clothing and the height and approximately what I thought might have been their weight. I couldn't tell you much more. I couldn't tell them much more.

Q Pardon me, sir?

A I couldn't tell them much more.

Q Did the officers ask you at that time when they were questioning you to tell them as much as you could?

A Yes, sir, I did as much as I could.

Q Did you close your business at the regular time that night, sir?

A Yes, I did.

MR. PARRISH: Objection to relevance.

THE COURT: Sustained.

MR. XINOS: I will tie it up.

THE COURT: Subject to tying it up.

MR. XINOS: Q Prior to the time you closed your business did you leave your place of business?

A Yes, I did.

Q Where did you go, sir?

A As Mr. Payne and the other lad ran out I chased them—

Q I mean after the police arrived.

A This was before the police arrived.

Q After the police arrived, excuse me, did you leave your place of business?

A No, I didn't.

Q Did you have the occasion to go to a police station in the city of Chicago after you closed your place of business and before noon on the following day?

A After I closed my business they called me during the middle of the night to go to the station for a lineup.

Q And did you go then to the station?

A Yes, I did.

Q And then did you return home?

A Yes.

Q And then shortly thereafter you went to the station again, is that correct?

A The next day.

Q Do you remember approximately what time you went to the station the second day or the second time?

A The second time was for a two o'clock showup.

Q Two o'clock in the afternoon?

A   Yes, sir.

Q   How were you notified that you were
to come or how were you asked to come to
the station?

A   I was called.

Q   Do you know which officer called you?

A   I believe it was Officer Higgins but
I'm not positive.

Q   Do you recall at that time what the
officer told you about coming to the station and why you should come down?

MR. PARRISH: Objection.

THE WITNESS: Because they felt they had
the man.

THE COURT: He may answer.

MR. XINOS: Q   Say that again, sir.

A   They felt they had the man, that is
all, nothing else.

Q   And did you go down to the station
at that time, is that correct?

A   Yes.

Q   Is that with Mr. DeAngelo or—

A   Yes.

Q   Did you pick him up?

A   We went together, sir.

Q   And it was at that time that you saw
Donald Payne in the police station?

A   Yes.

Q   Is that correct?

A   Yes.

Q   Prior to August of 1970, had you ever
seen Mr. Payne before?

A   No, sir.

Q   Have you discussed this event, this
attempt armed robbery, with your employee,
Mr. DeAngelo?

A There is not much to discuss with him. He was right there.

Q I mean have you talked about it between the time it happened and say today?

A Well, we talked about it.

Q Did you come to court together?

A Yes, sir.

MR. XINOS: Thank you, sir.

MR. PARRISH: One moment.

REDIRECT EXAMINATION
BY MR. PARRISH:

Q At the time that you were at the police district the next day, August 5, 1970, when you saw Donald Payne was he alone or with some other person?

A He was in a lineup, sir.

Q And about how many men were there in that lineup?

A At least—

Q About how many people were in that lineup other than Donald Payne?

A At least five.

Q And were they all black people?

A Yes, sir.

Q Were they of similar build and height as Donald Payne?

A More or less, sir.

Q Were they of similar color and complexion as Donald Payne?

A They were all similar, sir.

Q And you identified Donald Payne on that day in question, did you not?

A Yes, I did, sir.

Q Is there any doubt in your mind now as you sit here in court that Donald Payne is not the person on August 4, 1970, that held up—that held a gun and attempted to kill you?

A   Donald Payne is the man that fired the gun at me, sir.

MR. PARRISH: Thank you, sir.

> (Witness excused.)

THE COURT: We will take a five-minute recess, ladies and gentlemen.

> (Thereupon a recess was taken after which the following pro-ceedings were had within the presence and hearing of the jury.)

THE COURT: Call the next witness.

MR. PODUSKA: Officer Higgins.

> JOSEPH HIGGINS,

a witness called on behalf of the People, having been first duly sworn, was ex-amined and testified as follows:

DIRECT EXAMINATION
BY MR. PODUSKA:

Q   Sir, would you state your name?

A   Joseph Higgins.

Q   And what is your present occupation, sir?

A   Police officer for the city of Chicago.

Q   Directing your attention back to the evening of August 4 of 1970, where were you employed on that date?

A   City of Chicago, 6th District.

Q   And what was your assignment in the 6th District, sir?

A   Tactical Unit.

Q   And the evening of August 4, 1970, were you riding in a police car?

A Yes, sir, I was.

Q Was it a marked or unmarked police car?

A An unmarked one.

Q And on the evening of August 4 of 1970 were you riding in that car alone at approximately nine o'clock or were you with somebody else?

A I had my partner with me, Officer Cullen.

Q Similarly assigned to that district?

A Yes, sir.

Q And you were on routine patrol, is that correct?

A Yes, sir.

Q Did anything unusual occur?

A Yes, it did. We were stopped by Mr. Castelli in front of his place of business.

Q Was that liquor store open or closed at that time?

A It was opened.

Q Was it light or dark outside at that time?

A It was dark out.

Q Was the store lit or dark at that time?

A The store had lights on inside.

Q You say you were stopped in front of the store?

A Yes, sir.

Q What did you do upon being stopped?

A We talked to Mr. Castelli and he stated—

MR. XINOS: Objection.

THE COURT: Sustained.

MR. PODUSKA: Q When you say "we" who are you speaking of?

A   My partner and myself talked to Mr. Castelli.

Q   Who was present at that time?

A   Mr. Castelli and Mr.—we went inside the store with Mr. Castelli and Mr. DeAngelo.

Q   Approximately what place inside this store did this conversation occur?

A   As you come in the door he had a counter there where they sold liquor and right by the counter.

Q   Would you speak up a little louder because I'm having a hard time hearing you.

A   As you walk into the store there is a counter directly to your left and approximately there is where we had the conversation about five feet or ten feet inside the door.

Q   Was there anyone else in the store other than you, your fellow officer, and Mr. Castelli and his employee at that time?

A   There might have been some customers in there. I do not know.

Q   Did the customers take any part whatsoever in the conversation?

A   No, sir, they did not.

Q   Did any of the customers stand and listen to the conversation for any substantial length of time?

A   No, sir.

Q   Approximately what time did that conversation occur?

A   Approximately nine-fifteen to nine-twenty in the evening.

Q   What, if anything, did you say to

Mr. Castelli and what, if anything, did
he say in return?

MR. XINOS: Objection, Your Honor.

THE COURT: Sustained.

MR. PODUSKA: Q What did you say to
Mr. Castelli if anything?

MR. XINOS: Objection—

THE WITNESS: He informed us—

THE COURT: Sustained.

MR. PODUSKA: Q You had a conversation
with Mr. Castelli?

A Yes, sir, I did.

Q Do you recall at that time what the
conversation consisted of?

A Yes, sir, that the robbery had—attempted robbery had taken place in his
store approximately fifteen to twenty
minutes before—

MR. XINOS: Objection, Your Honor.

THE COURT: Sustained.

MR. PODUSKA: Q After that conversation
what, if anything, happened?

A We proceeded on the street to look
for an automobile with a license number
that was involved in the attempted
robbery—

MR. XINOS: Objection to that.

THE COURT: Sustained as to the volun-
teered statement, the portion of it—

MR. XINOS: I ask the jury be instructed
to disregard that portion.

THE COURT: The jury will be instructed
to disregard that portion.

MR. PODUSKA: Q Officer, at a subsequent time in the evening of August 4 of
1970 did you have occasion to come in

contact with an individual by the name of
James Robinson?

A   I came into contact with him.

MR. XINOS: Objection, the question
calls for a yes or no answer.

THE COURT: Sustained.

MR. PODUSKA: Q   Yes or no, did you have
occasion to come in contact with a James
Robinson?

A   Yes, I did.

Q   Officer, subsequent to leaving Shop-
Rite Liquors, Chicago, on the evening of
August 4 of 1970, did you have occasion to
come in contact with a Frank Robinson?

A   Before I left—I misunderstood you,
Counsel.

Q   I will rephrase the question. Officer, subsequent to going to the address of
Shop-Rite Liquors, Chicago, Illinois, on
August 4 of 1970, approximately nine,
nine-thirty, subsequent to that did you
have occasion to come in contact with a
James Robinson?

A   No, sir.

Q   Did you have occasion to come in contact with a Frank Robinson?

A   Not at that time.

Q   Did you have occasion to come in contact with either of those gentlemen?

MR. XINOS: Objection on the ground of
relevancy, Judge, at this point.

THE COURT: Sustained at this time.

MR. PODUSKA: Q   Officer, in the morning
hours of August 5, 1970, did you have
occasion to accompany certain other officers to the location of the home of Frank
Robinson?

A Yes, I did.

Q And approximately what time was that?

A Approximately seven-thirty in the morning of the fifth.

Q And Officer, do you recall the names of anyone who accompanied you?

A There was Officer Krueger of Area 2, Officer Jackson of Area 2, and my partner Officer Cullen and Sergeant Edenfield of the 6th District.

Q Do you recall where you went?

A I believe the address would be West 104 Place.

Q In Chicago, Illinois, is that correct?

A Yes, sir.

Q What, if anything, did you find upon entering that address?

A We found Frank Robinson, placed him under arrest, and brought him into the 6th District.

Q Upon bringing him into the district did you have occasion to have any conversations with him?

A We had a conversation with him in the 6th District, in front of his father at that time too.

Q This was approximately what time?

A Approximately eight o'clock.

Q Eight o'clock in the morning on August 5?

A Yes, sir.

Q His father was present?

A Yes, sir.

Q He was present?

A Yes, sir.

Q Was anyone else present?

MR. XINOS: Object to the relevancy of this.

THE COURT: Sustained.

MR. PODUSKA: Q The conversation took place, is that correct?

A Yes, sir, it did.

Q After that conversation did you do anything?

A Yes, sir, we went to South 100th Street.

Q And what, if anything, occurred there?

A We placed the defendant, Donald Payne, under arrest.

Q At approximately what time of day was that?

A About eight-thirty, twenty minutes to nine in the morning of the fifth.

Q And what did you do with Donald Payne at that time?

A He was advised of his rights—

MR. XINOS: Objection.

THE COURT: Sustained.

MR. PODUSKA: Q Where was he taken, first of all?

A Into the 6th District.

Q Was there anyone else with him at that time?

A Just the arresting officers.

Q The arresting officers being whom?

A Officer Krueger, myself, Sergeant Edenfield, and my partner, Officer Cullen.

Q And Officer, before you had a conversation with Frank Robinson did you know the defendant's address—

MR. XINOS: Objection.

THE COURT: Sustained.

MR. PODUSKA: Your Honor, at this time I will tender the witness to defense counsel for cross-examination.

CROSS-EXAMINATION
BY MR. XINOS:

Q Is that Detective Higgins?

A No, Patrolman.

Q Officer Higgins, what area, what police area is the liquor store located in?

A It's located in the 6th Police District, Area 2.

Q And you are assigned to Area 2, is that correct?

A I'm assigned to the 6th District.

Q Does the defendant, Donald Payne, live in the 6th District, his address?

A No, sir.

Q Is that still in Area 2?

A Yes, sir, it is.

Q Are you generally familiar with that area, that is Area 2?

A Yes, sir.

Q Can you approximate in terms of blocks or miles as best you can the distance between the home of Donald Payne and Mr. Castelli's liquor store?

A Approximately forty blocks, four miles.

Q When you went to the home of Donald Payne early in the morning on the fifth were you armed with a search warrant or arrest warrant?

A No, sir, I was not.

Q How many officers entered Donald Payne's house?

A   I believe there was three of us that
entered the house.

Q   His house, is it an apartment building and Donald Payne has an apartment or
would you describe the kind of building
that it is?

A   It's a single dwelling house with
bedrooms—

Q   A two story?

A   Like a dormer style.

Q   Who allowed you into the house, if
you know?

A   I believe it was his sister.

Q   Once you got into the house where did
you go?

A   We asked where Donald was and she
said on the second floor.

Q   When you went to the second floor
what kind of room did you go into?

A   It's like an attic bedroom.

Q   And did you see Donald Payne in that
room?

A   Yes, sir.

Q   And what was his condition in the
room? What was he doing?

A   He was in bed.

Q   As far as you know up until the time
that you arrived had he been sleeping?

MR. PARRISH: Objection.

THE COURT: Sustained.

MR. XINOS: Q While you were in the
room, when you first saw Donald Payne in
the room, was he dressed or undressed?
By that I mean did he have street clothes
and shoes on or did he have something less
than that on?

A   He had something less than that on.

Q   And did you instruct Donald Payne to get dressed?

A   Yes, sir.

Q   Did you or your fellow officers in your presence search Donald Payne, his bed, and that bedroom?

A   Yes, sir.

Q   Who conducted the search? Was that you, sir?

A   I searched his clothes that he put on him.

Q   And who was it that searched the area around the place where he was arrested?

A   It was either Sergeant Edenfield or Officer Krueger.

Q   As far as you know was any other portion of the house searched?

A   No, sir, no other portion.

Q   To the best of your knowledge, Officer, was anything found either on the person of Donald Payne or in his bed or in his bedroom that would in any way implicate him or connect him with the robbery or the attempt robbery of Mr. Castelli's liquor store?

A   No, sir.

Q   Officer, when you arrived at Mr. Castelli's liquor store at about say nine-fifteen on the evening of the fourth did you have a conversation with him at that time?

A   Yes, sir, I did.

Q   Did you ask Mr. Castelli questions and did he respond to your questions?

A   Yes, sir, he did.

Q   And either at the time of the questions and answers or at some time immedi-

ately thereafter did you have occasion
to make out any kind of a police report
regarding this incident?

A Yes, we did.

Q I show you what has been marked as
Defendant's Exhibit No. 1 for identification consisting of two pages and ask you
if you have seen that before, sir?

A Yes, sir, I have.

Q And what does that purport to be
without going into details?

A That is the robbery case report made
out by my partner and myself.

Q It's a typewritten report, is that
correct?

A Yes, sir, it is.

Q Do you know now who executed this
report, that is who typed out this report?

A Officer Cullen.

Q Did you read this report?

A Yes, sir, I did.

Q Have you had any occasion to change
anything that is in this report from
the day that was typed up until the present time?

A No, sir.

Q As far as you know were any changes
made by Detective or Officer Cullen in
the report?

A Not to my knowledge.

Q When you interviewed Mr. Castelli in
his liquor store at about nine-fifteen
or nine-twenty that evening did you have
occasion to obtain from him a description
of the men or boys who were involved in
this attempted robbery of his establishment?

MR. PARRISH: Objection, Your Honor.

THE COURT: He may answer.

MR. XINOS: Q Did you, sir?

A He gave us a description. He gave us a description of what he could remember of the men.

Q And as a result of him giving you this description did you place any of this information or all of it or any part of it in your police report?

A Yes, sir.

Q Do you recall in your conversation with Mr. Castelli how he physically described the shorter of the two men insofar as height, weight, and whatever?

A I believe approximately five-foot-eight, about 135 pounds.

Q And do you recall if he gave you any further description of the shorter man other than that the man was a Negro?

A I think he said he was approximately in his early twenties.

Q Do you recall that he gave any other description other than that, of facial characteristics or hair or scars or anything like that, if you remember?

A I can't remember, no, sir.

Q I call your attention to the description given by Mr. Castelli of the taller of the two men that came into the store. Do you recall him giving you a description as to the taller man?

A About six foot one, neatly dressed, and weighed approximately 180, 185 pounds.

Q Do you recall without looking at your police report whether he told you 180 or 185 pounds?

A   When he showed me the report it was 185.

Q   A hundred eighty-five pounds?

A   Yes.

Q   Any other description?

A   Other than 185 pounds and the taller of the two robbers, age approximately nineteen to twenty-one, male Negro.

Q   Did Mr. Castelli indicate to you any of the facial characteristics that he may have noticed on either of the two men? By that I mean scars or pimples or any kind of birth marks, anything like that?

A   I can't recall, sir.

Q   Do you recall if Mr. Castelli indicated anything about growth of hair on the face of either of the two men? By that I mean sideburns, mustache, beard, anything to that effect?

A   I believe he said one of the men had his hair cut short.

Q   Do you recall now whether you recognized that in your police report?

A   I don't think it's in there, sir.

Q   Did you have the occasion to talk to Mr. DeAngelo at that time?

A   Yes, sir.

Q   What was Mr. DeAngelo—strike that. Did Mr. DeAngelo relate to you substantially the same information that was related to you by Mr. Castelli?

MR. PARRISH: Objection.

THE COURT: Sustained.

MR. XINOS: Q   Did you happen to make a report on your conversation with Mr. DeAngelo?

MR. PARRISH: Objection, Judge.

THE COURT: He may answer.

THE WITNESS: It's in with that report, Counsel.

MR. XINOS: Q All in the same report?

A Yes.

Q After talking with Mr. Castelli and Mr. DeAngelo you made out your report or indicated that the taller man in their opinion weighed 185 pounds, is that correct?

A I believe that to be correct, yes.

MR. XINOS: Thank you, sir. No further questions.

REDIRECT EXAMINATION
BY MR. PODUSKA:

Q Now Officer, in the report that Counsel just showed you contained your notes or your report of the conversation which occurred between you and Mr. Castelli, is that right?

A Yes, sir.

Q Now Officer, Counsel just asked you a few questions. Officer, what, if anything, did you say to Mr. Castelli and what did he say in response?

MR. XINOS: Objection unless the question is limited.

THE COURT: Sustained.

MR. PODUSKA: Q Officer, you went into the Shop-Rite Liquors on the evening of August 4, 1970?

A Yes, sir, I did.

Q Pursuant to being waved down in the street by Mr. Castelli?

A Yes, sir.

Q And you went up to him, was there
nyone else in the store at the time?

A Mr. DeAngelo and there might have
een customers in there, I don't know.

Q You had a conversation between your-
elf and Mr. Castelli, is that correct?

A Yes, sir.

Q Was Mr. DeAngelo standing there at
he time?

A Yes, sir.

Q Where this conversation occurred in
he store?

A By the liquor counter as you walk in
he front door.

Q Did you see any customers take part
n that conversation or hear any customers
ake part in that conversation?

MR. XINOS: Objection, asked and an-
wered. Outside the scope—

THE COURT: He may answer.

MR. PODUSKA: Q Officer, you just
estified in response to Counsel's ques-
ions as to the description that Mr.
astelli gave you of two male Negro indi-
iduals, one taller than the other, is
hat right?

A Yes, sir.

Q And you recorded that in your police
eport, is that right?

A Yes, sir.

Q Now of your own recollection what did
r. Castelli say in regard to the two
ndividuals that came into his store and
hat, if anything, did you say in re-
ponse?

MR. XINOS: Objection.

THE COURT: Sustained.

MR. PODUSKA: Q Officer, there was certain conversation between you and Mr. Castelli, is that correct?

A Yes, sir.

Q Was the conversation with respect to the description the only conversation you had with Mr. Castelli?

A No, sir.

Q And, Officer, was anything else said?

A Yes, sir.

Q What else was said, Officer?

MR. XINOS: Object to that, Judge.

THE COURT: Objection sustained.

MR. PODUSKA: At this time, Your Honor, the State will excuse this witness.

THE COURT: All right.

MR. XINOS: No further questions. Thank you, sir.

THE COURT: You may step down.

          (Witness excused.)

THE COURT: Ladies and gentlemen, we will recess until twelve o'clock noon tomorrow and I would admonish you not to in any manner discuss any of the testimony you have heard from the witness stand among yourselves or with any friends or relatives. Above all if any news media should in any manner cover or touch upon this case you are instructed to disregard it, and above all if anyone should endeavor to talk to you about the case you are instructed to immediately advise the Court. We will recess until twelve o'clock tomorrow.

        (Thereupon said cause was adjourned until the following day, Wednesday, December 16, 1970, at 12:00 o'clock P.M.)

THE PEOPLE OF THE)
STATE OF ILLINOIS)
)
    vs.   )
) Charge: Attempt
DONALD PAYNE   )   Robbery, Etc.
                Before Judge Richard
                J. Fitzgerald and a
                jury

                Wednesday, December
                16, 1970
                12:00 o'clock P.M.

    Court convened pursuant to adjourn-
ment.

    Present:
    MR. WALTER PARRISH and
    MR. JOSEPH PODUSKA,
        Assistant State's Attorneys,
        appeared for the People;
    MR. CONSTANTINE P. XINOS,
        Assistant Public Defender,
        appeared for the Defendant.

THE CLERK: People of the state of
Illinois versus Donald Payne.

MR. XINOS: Donald Payne is before the
Court, Judge. The Court is aware this
matter has proceeded to trial and we are
in the middle of the trial. Donald Payne
has asked me to ask this Court to engage
in a conference so I'm asking on his behalf. Is that correct, Donald?

THE DEFENDANT: Correct.

THE COURT: Mr. Payne, we are now in the
middle of the trial charging you with
attempt robbery and attempt murder. Your
counsel now advises me that you are asking him to permit him to engage in a
conference with the State's Attorney and
the Court and discuss the possibilities of
a plea and to discuss some aspects of
the case.

You realize that any conference and the
results of any conference the Court isn't
bound by any agreement that might be
reached by the State's Attorney and your
counsel. However, if you are desirous
of having the Court and the State's Attorney and your counsel engage in a conference with the possibility of your plea
being discussed the Court will engage in
that conference. Is that your wish and
desire?

THE DEFENDANT: Yes.

THE COURT: Very well, we will pass it then for a conference.

MR. XINOS: Thank you, Judge.

> (After an interval of time, the following proceedings were had.)

THE CLERK: People of the State of Illinois versus Donald Payne.

MR. XINOS: Mr. Payne is before the Court, Judge. Pursuant to our conference I have advised Mr. Payne what the State would recommend in exchange for Mr. Payne's plea of guilty to both counts of the indictment and Mr. Payne at this time desires to change his plea from one of not guilty to one of guilty.

THE COURT: Is that correct, Mr. Payne?

THE DEFENDANT: Correct.

THE COURT: Before accepting your plea of guilty to the charges contained in the indictment, Mr. State's Attorney, would you kindly advise the Court as to what the facts are in this case.

MR. PARRISH: Judge, may it be stipulated by and between the People of the state of Illinois represented by the State's Attorney of Cook County, Edward V. Hanrahan, and the defendant in his own proper person, Donald Payne, represented by his attorney, Mr. Constantine Xinos, Assistant Public Defender, that if Mr. Joseph Castelli, spelled C-a-s-t-e-l-l-i, and Mr. Fred DeAngelo were called to testify either individually or collectively they would indicate that at about 9:10 P.M. on August 4, 1970, they were

both working then in the liquor store
in the city of Chicago.

That the defendant, Donald Payne, along
with one Frank Robinson who is presently
before the Court, Frank Robinson then being the age of approximately sixteen
years, went into that liquor store. That
the defendant, Donald Payne, pulled out a
gun, which was heretofore marked during
the course of a trial as People's Exhibit
No. 1 for identification, and pointed the
gun at the victim, Joseph Castelli, and
also Fred DeAngelo who were standing side
by side behind the counter.

Let it further be stipulated that Joseph
Castelli would say he was taking certain
money out of the cash register and transferring that to his pocket in preparation
for closing the store. That he had with
him in his possession between two and
three hundred dollars at that time.

Let it further be stipulated one Donald
Payne, while armed with a revolver, said
to Joe Castelli that "I want that." At
that time Joe Castelli began to back away
and the juvenile, Frank Robinson, ran
around at or near this location. At that
time Donald Payne with an outstretched
arm attempted to kill one Joseph Castelli
by pulling the trigger of People's Exhibit
No. 1, a small-caliber automatic weapon,
at least three or four times.

Subsequent to that time Mr. Castelli and
Mr. DeAngelo would testify that the two
persons, Frank Robinson and Donald Payne,
exited the store. They fled out of the

store and Mr. Joseph Castelli and Fred
DeAngelo pursued them.

They would further indicate individually
and collectively that some citizen came
into the store and indicated that he had
observed an automobile parked in a near
vicinity, obtained the license number of
that vehicle. That vehicle turned out to
be the vehicle owned or driven by one
James Robinson who is before the Court at
the present time.

Let it further be stipulated that a
trace of the license plate led to one
James Robinson who subsequently implicated
Frank Robinson, and subsequently Frank
Robinson accompanied certain police officers, to-wit Officers Higgins and Cullen
of the 6th District Tactical Unit and
Detective Jackson and Detective Krueger
who are present and available to testify
of Area 2 Robbery, and proceeded to the
home of the defendant, Donald Payne, at
South 100th Street in the city of Chicago
on August 5, 1970, and arrested the
defendant.

These officers would further indicate
that they obtained the weapon in the car
of the person named James Robinson through
their investigation.

Let it further be stipulated that Donald
Payne was placed in a lineup at about
2 P.M. on August 5, 1970, and he was
positively identified by Joseph Castelli
and Fred DeAngelo.

Let it further be stipulated that venue
is the state of Illinois, county of Cook,

city of Chicago, and the approximate age of this defendant is now—

MR. XINOS: Eighteen. So stipulated.

MR. PARRISH: Based upon the acceptance of the stipulated facts the State would rest its case in chief, Your Honor.

THE COURT: Mr. Payne, you have had an opportunity to discuss this case with your mother. You also have had an opportunity to discuss this case with your lawyer, have you?

THE DEFENDANT: Yes.

THE COURT: You realize that you have a right to persist in your plea of not guilty by entering a plea of not guilty and you have a right to persist in that plea, do you?

THE DEFENDANT: Yes.

THE COURT: Are you entering this plea voluntarily; there has been no threats, no coercion, no promises made to you other than the fact that the State has indicated they would recommend a sentence of one to five years to the Court, is that correct?

THE DEFENDANT: Yes.

THE COURT: Do you understand what you are charged with in this indictment?

THE DEFENDANT: Yes.

THE COURT: What is your understanding as to what you are charged with?

THE DEFENDANT: Attempt murder and attempt robbery.

THE COURT: You realize you also have a right to remain silent and not say anything to anybody, you understand that?

THE DEFENDANT: Yes.

THE COURT: You also realize that you have certain vested rights, that you have the right during the course of the trial to cross-examine witnesses. Your lawyer would proceed to enter into the procedure wherein he would cross-examine witnesses. You understand you have that right during the course of the trial, you understand?

THE DEFENDANT: Yes.

THE COURT: You realize that you also have a right to offer evidence on your own behalf to show you are not guilty of the charges contained in the indictment, you understand that?

THE DEFENDANT: Yes.

THE COURT: You also are presumed to be innocent of the charges contained in the indictment and that presumption of innocence remains with you all during the course of the trial. The State has an obligation of proving you guilty beyond a reasonable doubt.

When you enter a plea of guilty to the charges contained in this indictment the State is no longer obligated to prove you guilty of anything because you are in effect confessing the crime charged and that presumption of innocence that you are clothed with also automatically falls. Do you understand that?

THE DEFENDANT: Yes.

THE COURT: I also advise you that on your plea of guilty to the two counts contained in the indictment, on Count One of this indictment charging you with attempt robbery you may be sentenced to the

Illinois State Penitentiary for not less
than one nor more than fourteen years.

On your plea of Count Two of this indictment charging you with attempt murder
you may be sentenced to the Illinois State
Penitentiary for a period of not less
than one nor more than twenty years.

Knowing all of these facts and knowing
all of these admonitions that the Court
has given you, do you still persist in
your plea of guilty?

THE DEFENDANT: Yes.

THE COURT: Let the record show that the
defendant has been advised of the conse-
quences of his plea of guilty to the
charges contained in this indictment and
after having been so advised the defendant
persists in his plea. The plea, there-
fore, will be accepted and there will be
a finding of guilty of attempt murder and
attempt robbery in the manner and form as
charged in the Indictment and there will
be a judgment on the finding.

We will now proceed in hearing in aggravation and mitigation to determine what
the sentence should be.

MR. PARRISH: May it please the Court,
the defendant has the following criminal
history: On November 12, 1969, for
burglary the defendant was placed on two
years' probation with the first fifteen
days to be served in the House of Correction by Judge Landesman.

Other than the circumstances involved in
this indictment wherein the defendant
attempted to kill a citizen, against the
peace and dignity of the People of the

State of Illinois, the People offer no
further aggravation but recommend he be
sentenced to the penitentiary for not less
than one nor more than five years as to
each count.

THE COURT: Mitigation?

MR. XINOS: In mitigation I advise the
Court that the background of Mr. Payne,
he is eighteen, he was born in Chicago,
lived here all his life, currently resides
on the far South Side with his mother who
has been in court every time this matter
has been up and also his stepfather. He
has three brothers and two sisters.

In 1968 Donald Payne left high school
and went to work. Since that time he has
worked steady as a construction worker,
in a printing company. He worked for
Zenith Radio Corporation up to the truck
strike and worked for the Drake Hotel.
At the time of his arrest he was unem-
ployed.

He has never been married, never been in
the armed forces. He has taken, I think,
a big step toward rehabilitation in real-
izing the course of the trial that perhaps by admitting his guilt, he could
better adjust himself to society when he
gets out. I have nothing further in mitigation. I concur in the recommendation.

THE COURT: Mr. Payne, in view of the
recommendation made by the State and the
facts tendered in aggravation, it will be
the judgment of this Court that you be
sentenced to the Illinois State Penitentiary for a period of not less than one
nor more than five years.

I am taking into consideration the fact that you are eighteen years of age, that you do have a good background, and I feel that there is some possibility that giving of a short span of time in the Illinois State Penitentiary you can go down there, at least try to rehabilitate yourself, and get into a trade down there. This is the first real brush that you have had with the law.

You can go down to the State Penitentiary and you can be antagonistic to the authorities down there and you may stay there in the penitentiary for as long as five years. If you enter into the penitentiary with a spirit of true repentance, with the understanding that you are going to cooperate, with the understanding that you are going to try to do something for yourself, you could come out of that penitentiary with some fixed type of trade, but if you want to go down there and do nothing at all and sit on your haunches and do nothing and not cooperate and do nothing for yourself then you will come back out here and you will probably be facing in the next couple of years and you will probably be going down there for twenty or thirty years.

Now it's entirely up to you. You are at the crossroad. You are young, you can either spend the rest of your life down in the penitentiary or you can resolve yourself into doing something for yourself.

I am giving you the first break you probably ever got in your life. With the

type of charges that are against you you
could go down to the penitentiary for ten
to twenty years. You are going down there
from one to five years which means at the
end of eleven months that the Parole Board
can take a look at you and see whether or
not you are rehabilitated, whether or
not you can come back into society. You
may not be quite that fortunate the next
time. So I strongly urge you that you
have gotten a break because people have
confidence in you and you feel you can do
something with yourself. So the rest of
it, Donald, is up to you. Do you understand that?

THE DEFENDANT: Yes.

THE COURT: I further advise you you
have a right to appeal from the judgment
of the Court. In the event that you are
desirous of appealing and you are without
funds with which to engage counsel, free
counsel will be appointed to represent
you. I would also instruct the Clerk of
the Circuit Court of Cook County, Criminal
Division, to provide you with a free
transcript of these proceedings to aid
and assist you in any appeal you might be
desirous of making.

I would also instruct the Clerk of the
Circuit Court of Cook County, Criminal
Division, to provide you with a free transcript of the proceedings and to aid and
assist you he will file a notice of appeal
on your behalf.

I only say now get down there and behave
yourself and let's make something of
yourself. Are you satisfied with the

counsel you have had and the representa-
tion you have had?

THE DEFENDANT: Yes, sir. One thing—

THE COURT: Yes, sir?

THE DEFENDANT: I would like an early
shipment.

THE COURT: We will send you on Friday.
Let the mittimus issue.

MR. XINOS: The agreement I have with
the State is that if the State seeks to
proceed on the probation violation the
State will recommend identical concurrent
time, is that correct?

MR. PARRISH: That is absolutely correct.

MR. XINOS: Motion defendant mistrial.

THE COURT: Allowed. Bring out the
jury, please.

> (Thereupon the following pro-
> ceedings were had within the
> presence and hearing of the
> jury.)

THE COURT: Ladies and gentlemen of the
jury, at this time I will advise you that
the defendant in this case has withdrawn
his plea of not guilty and has entered
a plea of guilty to the charges contained
in the indictment, so it will be un-
necessary for you to remain in our courtroom and deliberate on the charges. However, I would like to thank you for your
patience and your cooperation in this
matter. You have been most attentive and
very diligent in the duties that you have
assumed.

Sometimes during the course of these
trials the defendants withdraw their pleas

and enter a plea such as we have had in
this case. I assure you that evidently
your sterness as jurors has persuaded the
defendant to enter a plea of guilty so
you can certainly feel that your work has
certainly been of some avail, and I hope
that between now and the time that you
complete your jury service you will have
an opportunity of going through the complete trial. And I assure you and want
to thank you for your services here in my
courtroom. So you will be excused and
the bailiff will take you back down into
the jury room. Thank you very much,
ladies and gentlemen.

      (Which were all the proceedings
      had in the above entitled
      cause.)

STATE OF ILLINOIS)
) SS.
COUNTY OF C O O K)

We, Joseph X. Tournier and Nathan
Shapiro, Official Court Reporters of the
Circuit Court of Cook County, County Department—Criminal Division, do hereby
certify that we reported in shorthand the
above proceedings had in the aforemen-
tioned cause, pending in said court on
these dates; that we thereafter tran-
scribed into typewriting the foregoing
transcript, which we hereby certify is a
true and correct transcript of such proceedings had in said cause.

(signed) Joseph X. Tournier
         Nathan Shapiro
         Official Court Reporters,
         Circuit Court of Cook County,
         County Department—Criminal
         Division.